The Archers

THE ARCHERS: AN UNOFFICIAL COMPANION

Copyright © Summersdale Publishers Ltd 2011

Text written by Sarah Herman.

Illustrations by Chichester Graphic Arts

Summersdale Publishers Ltd
46 West Street
Chichester
West Sussex
PO19 1RP
UK

www.summersdale.com

Printed and bound by CPI Group (UK) Ltd, Croydon, CR0 4YY

ISBN: 978-1-84953-178-8

Disclaimer
This book is unofficial and is not endorsed by or in any other way connected with the programme – it is written for fans by fans of the show. Every effort has been made to ensure that all information is correct. Should there be any errors, we apologise and shall be pleased to make the appropriate amendments in any future edition.

Substantial discounts on bulk quantities of Summersdale books are available to corporations, professional associations and other organisations. For details telephone Summersdale Publishers on (+44-1243-771107), fax (+44-1243-786300) or email (nicky@summersdale.com).

The Archers

AN UNOFFICIAL COMPANION

ROSIE DILLON

summersdale

Introduction

'Well, me old pal, me old beauty,' were the soon-to-be legendary words that Walter Gabriel chortled on Whit Monday, 29 May 1950. As the programme began its five-day pilot run the now familiar tune of 'Barwick Green' introduced the Midlands to the Archer family and the minutiae of their rural lives. Over sixty years later, *The Archers* is the longest-running drama serial of all time, anywhere in the world, and continues to draw almost five million listeners every week in the UK alone.

While it just recounts the lives of ordinary country folk from Ambridge, this hasn't stopped fans tuning in for five or, in recent years, six episodes every week to keep up to date with their favourite farmers. From dramatic births and deaths, love affairs and violent crimes to foot-and-mouth, farm sales, business ventures, cricket matches and village fêtes, Ambridge life is anything but dull. The commitment to lengthy storylines and the longevity of families and characters makes the programme's depiction of rural life realistic, but also entertaining and often gripping and moving for listeners.

But mainly it's the humdrum everyday life of the Ambridge villagers that keeps us coming back for more. And for many fans 7 p.m. just wouldn't be the same without a drink at The Bull, a chat in the kitchen at Brookfield Farm or the gentle moo of a cow grazing on open pasture. And who could imagine summer without the stalls of the village fête, September without knowing who's grown the best beans for the Flower and Produce Show and the build-up to Christmas without Lynda Snell plotting another theatrical extravaganza?

From the farms, families, deaths, dramas, animals and community antics, this book is a trip down a country memory lane and a delightful compendium of facts and frolics of *Archers* life. Find out what goes on behind the scenes and test your knowledge of Britain's best-loved radio drama with the themed quizzes throughout the book. Now, raise a pint of Shire's to sixty more years of Ambridge, turn the page and start reading.

Welcome to Ambridge: Ambridge Hall

✧ Ambridge Hall was originally built as the home for the village doctor.

✧ Erected in the 1860s, the Hall is built from yellow brick, has six bedrooms and a garden that extends down to the River Am.

✧ Laura Archer originally left Ambridge Hall to her lodger Colonel Danby in her will, but never signed the top copy of the will, so it was sold off to the Snells.

✧ The Snells decided to transform their home into a guest house; it is decorated – naturally – using the principles of feng shui.

✧ Lynda Snell has developed the gardens so they are now full of low-allergen plants, including a Shakespearean plot that only features plants named in the works of the Bard, in a possibly unconscious but wholly appropriate homage to E. F. Benson's Lucia. She was delighted when Matthew Wilson visited the garden to record a special feature for *Gardeners' Question Time* in early 2011.

How it all Began

✧ In the first five pilot episodes of *The Archers* airing just in the Midlands in Whit Week, 1950, the Archer family worked on Wimberton Farm, on the fringe of the village of Ambridge. Wimberton Farm was changed to Brookfield Farm for the trial three-month run, broadcast nationally from 1 January 1951.

✧ The original idea for the programme came from well-known Lincolnshire farmer Henry Burtt at a meeting between the BBC and farming representatives when he announced: 'What we need is a farming *Dick Barton*.' *Dick Barton* was an adventure serial surrounding the exploits of a secret agent.

✧ Up until 1962, almost every one of the 3,000 *Archers* episodes was written by *Dick Barton* scriptwriters Geoffrey Webb or Edward J. Mason.

✧ The programme was originally made for £47 per episode.

✧ Original editor Godfrey Baseley used to invite senior figures from the farming world to appear as themselves on the programme. In 1961 Sir Richard Trehane, chairman of the Milk Marketing Board, visited Ambridge and stayed as a guest of Charles Grenville and Carol Grey.

✧ Originally, cast members were paid varying amounts due to budget constraints – between £9 and £12 a week – but to avoid disputes they were led to believe they were all receiving the same fee. This wasn't kept a secret for long and Norman Painting (Phil Archer) was quick to voice his complaints when he discovered he was earning £2 less each week than Harry Oakes (Dan Archer).

✧ An introductory programme to ease listeners into *The Archers* before it started airing nationally was produced by Godfrey Baseley and transmitted in December 1950. The programme featured Godfrey visiting 'Ambridge' in a 'mobile recording vehicle' and talking to the characters as if they were real. He had a cup of tea at Brookfield Farm and commented on the possibility of a romance between Phil and Grace. The programme ended with Godfrey inviting listeners to come and eavesdrop some more on these country folk in January 1951.

✧ Within weeks of the first national episodes airing the programme had an audience of two million.

✧ Representatives from the Ministry of Agriculture and Fisheries (now the Department for Environment, Food and Rural Affairs) and the National Farmers' Union were on the programme's original advisory team, helping writers to include factual and informative farming messages.

Ambridge Issues: Organic vs GM

On 2 April 1984 milk quotas were introduced into the EU for farms producing milk or other milk products to try and restrain the rise in milk production. In Ambridge this saw Brookfield Farm reduce its dairy herd from 110 to 95 to comply with the quota it was set. The milk quotas gave Tony and Pat Archer the incentive they needed to turn Bridge Farm organic. By reducing their dairy herd they were able to let their full-time worker Malcolm Lewis go and dedicate more funds and time to cutting out artificial fertilisers, herbicides and pesticides. They made a commitment to converting 30 acres a year over five years and in 1985 they grew 10 acres of organic wheat, carrots and potatoes. By 1989 they were able to declare themselves fully organic and apply for Soil Association status. The storyline was inspired by a scriptwriter's visit to Brynllys Farm in Ceredigion, Wales, the UK's first certified organic dairy farm.

When Brian Aldridge received hefty subsidy cheques for Home Farm in the 1990s, Tony and Pat were jealous – subsidies for organic farmers were considerably less – but proud of their achievements. But in 1999 their younger son Tom was so outraged by the introduction of GM oil seed rape on Brian's land that he destroyed the crop and faced criminal charges. This was a realistic reflection of the disputes between organic and GM producers going on in the countryside. Two years after Tony Blair's 1997 election promised to introduce licences for experimental farming and reduce anti-GM hysteria, producers and consumers were still battling it out. While some farmers embraced GM crops and regarded dissenters as 'anti-science', organic farmers were concerned that modified organisms would cross-pollinate with natural species once in the soil, changing them irreversibly for the future.

There was no denying the success of organic farming with sales of organic products in the UK increasing from £100 million in 1993/4 to £1.21 billion in 2004, and Bridge Farm has reflected this growth with Pat expanding her dairy business from yogurt to ice cream and securing a lucrative contract with Underwoods, the Borchester department store. They now have their own farm shop in Borchester, 'Ambridge Organics', where among the array of organic offerings their daughter Helen's well-known cheeses are sold.

Quiz Night at The Bull:

What's on in Ambridge?

1 Which Ambridge event is celebrated on or around 21 October?
2 Where did the fireworks take place to mark the Queen's Coronation in 1953?
3 In 2003 which event saw the residents of Ambridge raise £300 for the church?
4 What was the name of the original donkey used at Ambridge's Palm Sunday services before Benjamin took his place?
5 Which well-known star of *The Dam Busters* cut the ribbon at the village fête in 1962?
6 Which popular literary character did Daniel Hebden Lloyd dress up as for Halloween in 2001?
7 Who co-produced 2003's Ambridge Mystery Plays with Lynda Snell?
8 At which event is the Lawson-Hope Cup presented?
9 Who was crowned Miss Ambridge at the 1977 Ambridge Fête, despite being from Penny Hassett?
10 In which country did Bert and Freda Fry spend Valentine's Day in 2006?

1 Apple Day; 2 Lakey Hill; 3 Harvest Supper; 4 Basil; 5 Richard Todd; 6 Harry Potter; 7 Reverend Alan Franks; 8 The Flower and Produce Show; 9 Ellen Padbury; 10 India

Family Facts: The Archers of Brookfield Farm

✧ Jill was wearing a yellow dress when Phil spotted her for the first time at the fête in 1957.

✧ Phil served as a JP on the Borchester Bench and was chairman of the local NFU.

✧ In 1982 Kenton Archer held the rank of Second Officer in the Merchant Navy.

✧ Mel Archer called from Australia to tell in-laws Phil and Jill that she had married their son Kenton.

✧ David Archer failed his mathematics A level twice.

✧ Ruth did not promise to 'obey' David in her marriage vows made in 1988.

✧ Philippa Rose Archer, known by all as Pip, was named after her granddad Phil and her Aunt Rose.

✧ Benjamin David Archer was born at home at Brookfield Farm on Eddie Grundy's birthday.

Welcome to Ambridge: Arkwright Hall

✧ The Hall is situated in Grey Gables Country Park by its own lake.

✧ While the house is Victorian, its foundations date back as early as the seventeenth century.

✧ After Charles Grenville bought the building in 1959 John Tregorran supervised its renovation and saw it transformed into a community centre.

✧ Before Jack Woolley became the Hall's new owner in 1965, the youth-orientated Cellar Club (opened in 1963) provided a soundproofed room for bands to play and kept the building in use.

✧ The Hall has been a leisure centre and a field studies centre, but was left unoccupied for many years. It has since been renovated by the Landmark Trust and serves as distinctive holiday accommodation.

14

Quiz Night at The Bull:

Bites and pieces

1 On what day of the week is the twice-monthly Borchester Farmers' Market held?
2 Whose stag night took place on Shrove Tuesday in 1994?
3 In which month of the year does Marmalade Making traditionally take place?
4 What did Walter Gabriel name his village fête ventriloquist's dummy?
5 Who hosted a ghost walk that began at The Bull in 2008?
6 What variety of apple, bought from a supermarket, stumped Lynda Snell in an identification contest on 2005's Apple Day?
7 Who challenged Alistair to the Three Peaks Challenge in 2003?
8 Tom Forrest formed the Ambridge branch of a shooting club in 1953 to hunt which animal?
9 Who was the WI's representative at the National Energy Conference in 1978?
10 What year did the village fête host its own Bushtucker Trials?

1 Thursday; 2 Robin Stokes's; 3 January; 4 Marmaduke; 5 Joe Grundy; 6 Pink Lady®; 7 David Archer; 8 Grey squirrels; 9 Jennifer Aldridge; 10 2004

GONE BUT NOT FORGOTTEN:
MARK HEBDEN

Born: 20 February 1955
Died: 17 February 1994

If any Ambridge couple could be said to have taken their time to 'get it together', Mark Hebden and Shula Archer would be in line for the title. Despite proposing to her on New Year's Eve 1980, Mark didn't tie the knot with Shula until nearly five years later, and even then married life was hardly a smooth ride. While Mark was a good egg – Borchester Under-14 Judo Champion, hang-gliding and sky-diving enthusiast and passionate solicitor with promising career prospects – it took Shula some time to figure out he was the man for her. In the interim, Mark embarked on relationships with Jackie Woodstock (she proposed, but he ended it over accusations she was flirting with other men on a skiing holiday) who lived with him at Penny Hassett, and fiancée Sarah Locke – the blonde, bubbly daughter of the senior partner at law firm Locke and Martin. When that engagement went south, Mark took a job offer in Hong Kong to help him move on. Shula visited him there and on his return he proposed to her on Lakey Hill.

Unfortunately, their married life was no smoother than their courtship. They struggled to conceive a baby – Shula had an ectopic pregnancy, and eventually after battling her demons over her sister's abortion, they opted for IVF – and Mark's commitment to his work put a lot of strain on the relationship. After a stint working in Birmingham he moved a lot closer to home setting up a practice in Borchester with Usha Franks (then Gupta) as his partner. Before his death he took on the controversial case of defending Susan Carter when she was accused of hiding her fugitive brother Clive. Tragically, Mark never did learn the wonderful news that his wife's second shot at IVF had been successful. On 17 February 1994, a few days shy of his thirty-ninth birthday, Mark was driving home when a reckless driver overtook him on a blind bend – he swerved to avoid horse rider Caroline Bone whose horse had thrown her to the ground, and ploughed into a tree. He died instantly and missed the birth of his longed-for son Daniel and what could have been many happy years together with Shula.

★ Famous Faces in Ambridge ★

It may be a small rural community nestled near the Hassett Hills, but that hasn't stopped some big names popping round for a visit. In fact a number of well-known faces, or rather, voices, have appeared as themselves on the programme over the last sixty years mingling with the good country folk of Ambridge.

✧ The annual fête in 1952, held on the last Saturday in June, was opened by **Gilbert Harding**. The journalist and *What's My Line?* panellist had worked with *Archers* creator Godfrey Baseley on some of his earlier farming programmes.

✧ Band leader **Humphrey Lyttelton** showed up in Ambridge in 1957 to open the church fête to raise money for the roof. The humorous jazz musician delivered a speech poking fun at the vicar and his 'outlaws' trying to take money from the rich to help the poor church roof!

✧ After Dan Archer bumped into World War Two army veteran and *Dam Busters* actor **Richard Todd** at a National Dairy Farmers' lunch, he persuaded him to stop by the village to open the 1962 village fête. Much to 17-year-old Jennifer Archer's delight her grandfather invited the actor for a drink at The Bull, even if she did have to listen to them talking about farming.

◆ Ambridge hosted its first royal visit in 1984 when **Princess Margaret** made an appearance as herself. She was attending the Borsetshire NSPCC Centenary Fashion Show held at Grey Gables – the charity of which she was president. Her part was recorded at Kensington Palace, where the Princess was concerned about noise being made by plumbers and the sound of a ticking clock in the room.

◆ When Robert and Lynda Snell went to see **Dame Edna Everage** at the theatre in 1988 they found themselves sitting so close to the front that Lynda found herself being addressed by Dame Edna herself and becoming the butt of some of Edna's jokes, although Lynda thought it was in fact *she* who had upstaged the international comedienne. The scene was shot in the Birmingham Hippodrome in front of the real audience of the programme and most of what was said was improvised.

Welcome to Ambridge: Blossom Hill Cottage

✧ This idyllic cottage is situated on a side road off the Borchester Road making it slightly removed from the rest of the village.

✧ It's been owned by Mike Daly, John Tregorran, Ralph and Lilian Bellamy, Peggy Archer and current owner Usha Franks.

✧ The two-bedroom house was used by Kate Aldridge and her gang of teenage friends to hang out.

✧ It's survived a burglary, a fire and an attack by racist vandals who sprayed offensive graffiti, targeted at Usha Franks (then Gupta), on its walls in 1995.

Borsetshire Birthdays

Do you share a birthday with any of the current crop of Ambridge residents? Check out the dates below.

2 *January*   Henry Archer
7 *January*   Jennifer Aldridge
10 *January*   Pat Archer
21 *January*   Brenda Tucker
30 *January*   Kathy Perks

2 *February*   Roy Tucker
9 *February*   Will Grundy
16 *February*   Tony Archer
17 *February*   Pip Archer
25 *February*   Tom Archer

7 *March*   Abbie Tucker
15 *March*   Ben Archer
15 *March*   Eddie Grundy
30 *March*   James Bellamy

3 *April*   Caroline Sterling
5 *April*   Robert Snell
7 *April*   George Grundy
16 *April*   Helen Archer
21 *April*   Elizabeth Pargetter

1 *May*   Hayley Tucker
12 *May*   Clarrie Grundy
22 *May*   Neil Carter
29 *May*   Lynda Snell

16 *June*   Ruth Archer
17 *June*   Usha Franks
19 *June*   Fallon Rogers
22 *June*   Christopher Carter
22 *June*   Adam Macy
28 *June*   Phoebe Aldridge

8 *July*   Lilian Bellamy
19 *July*   Jack Woolley
20 *July*   Jamie Perks

7 *August*   Matt Crawford
7 *August*   Emma Grundy
8 *August*   Kenton Archer
8 *August*   Shula Hebden Lloyd

13 *September*   Josh Archer
18 *September*   David Archer
18 *September*   Joe Grundy
28 *September*   Ed Grundy
29 *September*   Alice Carter
30 *September*   Kate Madikane

3 *October*   Jill Archer
10 *October*   Susan Carter

9 *November*   Clive Horrobin
11 *November*   Brian Aldridge
13 *November*   Peggy Woolley
14 *November*   Ruairi Donovan
14 *November*   Daniel Hebden Lloyd

1 *December*   Mike Tucker
12 *December*   Lily and Freddie Pargetter
21 *December*   Christine Barford
24 *December*   Debbie Aldridge

Making *The Archers*: The voices behind the villagers

The creator of *The Archers*, radio producer Godfrey Baseley, insisted on using a mixture of professional actors and 'normal' people in the recording of the programme. He believed that only with this injection of real-life country-dwellers and senior figures from the farming world would the necessary authenticity be achieved. Some of the programme's best-loved characters have emerged from this casting philosophy and have lived a slice of *Archers* life for real. For example, Bob Arnold (who played Tom Forrest) grew up in the Cotswolds, where his own father ran a village pub. He worked as a butcher and painted white lines on the roads of Oxfordshire before appearing in a BBC programme about the Cotswolds, which led to more appearances on BBC Midlands programmes and variety shows where he was known as 'Bob Arnold – The Farmer's Boy'.

With a regular cast of about sixty characters, working on *The Archers* is by no means a full-time job and even principal cast members only spend a few days a month in the recording studio. Because recording only takes place once every four weeks, and because not all cast members feature in every episode, actors are able to pursue other projects while their character remains on the show such as appearing in films, TV and stage work. Storylines are often written to accommodate these commitments – Debbie Aldridge runs a farm in Hungary so that when actress Tamsin Greig is not working on shows such as *Green Wing*, *Black Books* or *Episodes* she can pop back to Ambridge so Debbie can catch up with the family. Another advantage that *The Archers* has over rival TV serial dramas, where its actors are concerned, is that even if cast members decide to leave, or sadly pass away, it doesn't necessarily mean the end of the road for their characters. A number of Ambridge residents have been voiced by multiple actors over the years, perhaps most notably Dan Archer, who made it almost to the age of ninety thanks to the voices of four different men, and John Tregorran, who was voiced by five different actors on the programme.

Welcome to Ambridge: Bridge Farm

✧ Home to Pat and Tony Archer, Bridge Farm is an organic dairy farm, which produces yogurt, ice cream and cheese. The farm also has its own pigs and produces a range of vegetable crops.

✧ The family is particularly attached to their red-brick Victorian home on the farm.

✧ Bridge Farm converted to organic in 1984 and Pat and Tony received the coveted Soil Association symbol for their produce a year later.

✧ Pat and Tony's eldest son John died in a tractor accident in one of the farm's fields in 1998.

✧ The farm also supplies the Archer family's own shop in Borchester with their produce, including daughter Helen's Borsetshire Blue cheese.

✧ In 2008 Helen and her brother Tom encouraged their parents to buy the freehold of the 140-acre farm, which with the help of a large mortgage they were able to do.

Quiz Night at The Bull:

Charmed childhoods

1 Where was Susan Carter when her daughter Emma started wetting the bed in 1994?
2 When Christine passed her School Certificate what gift did Dan Archer give her to show how proud he was?
3 To get her son Daniel to eat carrots, Shula used to cut them into the shape of which animal?
4 Who was German au pair Eva Lenz hired to look after?
5 Where did Kate hold the naming ceremony for her daughter Phoebe?
6 Which one of Helen Archer's brothers preferred wearing a pair of her trousers than his own when he was six?
7 Which child has the longest name in Ambridge?
8 How old was Joe Grundy when he left school?
9 Who was Clive Horrobin's favourite superhero as a child?
10 Which teenager gave birth to baby Kylie (named after the Australian pop star) at the Vicarage in 1989?

1 Prison; 2 Bookcase; 3 Fish; 4 Kate Aldridge; 5 Lakey Hill; 6 Tom; 7 Daniel Mark Archer Hebden Lloyd; 8 Fourteen; 9 Superman; 10 Sharon Richards

Gone but not Forgotten:
Doris Archer

Born: 11 July 1890
Died: 26 October 1980

Dan Archer's right-hand woman was the domestic crutch that supported Brookfield Farm for many years while her husband worked the farm. From her time as a lowly kitchen maid and lady's maid to Letty Lawson-Hope, Doris Archer saw nothing wrong with spending her days tending to the farmhouse and cooking up all kinds of homemade delights. As the years passed in Ambridge, Doris became attached to her daughter-in-law Peggy and growing flock of grandchildren, especially Shula. Family played an enormous part in the life of this devoted woman, and while she may have struggled with the arrival of Dan's opinionated sister-in-law Laura Archer she was dedicated to the happiness of her own brother, Tom Forrest, who went through the wringer when he was charged with manslaughter. Sociable and friendly, Doris played an active role in village activities and was a founding member of the Ambridge WI – she even represented them at a Buckingham Palace garden party. Her Christian faith helped her through tough times, but caused conflict when her daughter Christine wished to remarry in St Stephen's, something she felt was inappropriate. Old age brought with it blood pressure problems, bad headaches and arthritis, but this delightful farmer's wife died peacefully in her chair at Glebe Cottage.

Family Facts: The Tuckers

✧ Mike Tucker lost the sight in one eye when he got hit by a hydraulic pipe, and he now wears an eye-patch.

✧ Betty Tucker came off the contraceptive pill without telling husband Mike before falling pregnant with Roy.

✧ Mike Tucker declared himself bankrupt in 1986, a low point in his life. Always an early riser, he's now happy in his role as Ambridge's milkman, working for the Grange Farm dairy.

✧ Brenda Tucker once worked as a trainee journalist on Radio Borsetshire.

✧ As a teenager, Roy Tucker was part of a racist gang that targeted Usha Franks (then Gupta).

✧ Betty shared her birthday with the Queen Mother.

✧ Hayley Tucker used to go out with John Archer before she got together with Roy – she and John met at the Ice House, a club in Birmingham.

✧ Hayley and Roy shared their first kiss on Millennium Eve on the village green. After a struggle to conceive, they were delighted to welcome baby Abbie into the family in 2008.

✧ Ballroom dancing has always been a big part of Mike's life. He and Betty used to tread the boards in village performances and he met his second wife Vicky at a dance class.

Welcome to Ambridge: Brookfield Bungalow

✧ This bungalow was originally built as a home for newly-weds Ruth and David Archer, who moved in on 12 September 1990.

✧ The home, situated in Little Field on Brookfield Farm, enjoys views of the river and has a garden.

✧ Ruth, David and family temporarily swapped homes with Phil and Jill Archer in 1999 when Jill injured her knee and found the bungalow's layout more suited to her recovery.

✧ Once Phil and Jill had moved permanently to Glebe Cottage, David and Ruth moved back into the main farmhouse. The bungalow provided an extra source of income as a holiday let, and then a home for Bert and Freda Fry.

Quiz Night at The Bull:

Furry, four-legged friends

1 What kind of animals did Lynda Snell bring to the church on Palm Sunday in 2003?
2 Who came up with the money-spinning fête attraction of performing seals Mutt and Jeff?
3 Whose horse is called Spearmint?
4 Which of the following animals is not a dog: Biff, Mitch, Tolly or Fly?
5 A peacock has been living at The Bull since 1993, but what is its name?
6 Who was known as 'the dog woman'?
7 Who tried to save Christine's horse Midnight from a stable fire, causing her own death in the attempt?
8 Ralph Bellamy commissioned a portrait of Lilian sitting on his horse – what was the horse's name?
9 Name the dog who tucked into Susan and Neil Carter's wedding cake in 1984.
10 Where are Majorie Antrobus's dogs Portia and Bettina buried?

1 Llamas; 2 Walter Gabriel; 3 Alice's; 4 Tolly; 5 Eccles; 6 Majorie Antrobus; 7 Grace Archer; 8 Red Knight; 9 Captain; 10 In the garden at Nightingale Farm

Family Facts: The Perkses

✧ Sid was a nineteen-year-old Brummie with a criminal record when he arrived in Ambridge in 1963. Jack Woolley took a shine to the boy from his homeland and gave him a job as his chauffeur and handyman for four years.

✧ Sid took pretty Bull barmaid Polly Mead out on a date to the Hollerton Fair in 1964 where his motorbike was stolen by thugs who knew him from his criminal past.

✧ As a child Lucy Perks wasn't allowed a puppy, so she imagined one called Crackers.

✧ Lucy went to Nottingham University to study ecological science, but never graduated because she was distracted by future husband Duncan Gemmell.

✧ For her wedding to Sid, Kathy wore a silk dress and a string of pearls she borrowed from Peggy.

✧ Jamie Perks was conceived after his parents had taken a moonlit stroll on the beach in New Zealand.

✧ Sid met Jolene Rogers at the gym in Borchester – it was Eddie Grundy who revealed their affair to Kathy in front of a full house at The Bull.

✧ Singer and landlady Jolene's real name is Doreen.

✧ When Kathy Perks and Kenton split up, Jamie Perks damaged the new bird hide at Arkwright Lake during a drunken gathering of his friends in his frustration.

GONE BUT NOT FORGOTTEN:
NIGEL PARGETTER

Born: 8 June 1959
Died: 2 January 2011

Nigel Pargetter died after falling off the roof of his beloved family home Lower Loxley Hall. At only fifty-one years old his departure will be felt by many, but especially by his wife Elizabeth and their eleven-year-old twins Lily and Freddie. Considered by some to have been born with a silver spoon in his mouth, the Rugby School-educated Nigel has not always had it as easy as other Ambridge residents may think. His carefree youth saw him enjoying life but unsuited to hard work – he tried being a swimming pool salesman, working on a beef and maize farm in Zimbabwe and even dabbling in the stock exchange during the 1980s. But it was the death of his father, and the subsequent responsibility of the Lower Loxley Hall estate landing on his shoulders that saw him finally grow up and take life a little more seriously.

The same could be said of his love life – an early interest in Shula Archer didn't amount to much, and he soon turned his attentions to her younger sister Elizabeth who he proposed to, although their immaturity saw the engagement broken and they went their separate ways. In 1992 Nigel hired Elizabeth to help him launch Lower Loxley Corporate Entertainments and together they began turning the decaying building and vast grounds into a profitable commercial enterprise. Brought closer by their work they married in 1994 and had their children in 1999. Nigel's mother Julia may not have approved of common folk using the family home for 'green weddings' and other events, but it's certainly turned the fortunes of the stately home around. It's heartbreaking that Nigel is no longer around to see the fruits of his labour thrive, or his children grow up.

Welcome to Ambridge: Brookfield Farm

◇ This 469-acre mixed farm has grown, shrunk and grown again over the years.

◇ Brookfield used to be part of a three-farm cooperative before it incorporated the holdings of Marney's and Hollowtree by the end of the 1960s.

◇ Brookfield was struck twice by TB in the 1990s.

◇ In 2001 David and Ruth Archer took over Brookfield when Phil retired and made the decision to contract out the arable farming to Home Farm.

◇ Despite bidding farewell to the pigs, the farm still boasts a 325-strong lambing flock. Brookfield lamb is marketed cooperatively under the Hassett Hills brand.

Quiz Night at The Bull:

Leave it up to fête

1 Who did Phil Archer spot and film at the village fête in 1957?

2 After learning of the existence of Ruairi Donovan, what did Alice throw in the bin on Father's Day?

3 In 2008 Lynda Snell attempted to outdo a production of which play put on by Larry Lovell ten years previously?

4 Who received a device for scraping ice off a car windscreen from her new husband for Christmas?

5 In 1994 residents hosted a ceremony to mark the twinning of Ambridge with which village in France?

6 Whose hand was burnt by a firework on Bonfire Night in 1991?

7 In 1965 a hypnotist at the village fête managed to convince farm worker Ned Larkin a glass of water he was drinking was filled with what?

8 Who suffered a heart attack at a car boot sale at Grange Farm in 1996?

9 Who gave a talk titled 'Agriculture in Australia' to the Ambridge WI?

10 Who received a medal from the British Legion for selling Remembrance poppies for over thirty years?

1 Jill Archer; 2 A Father's Day card she'd bought for Brian; 3 Jack and the Beanstalk; 4 Shula Hebden Lloyd; 5 Meyruelle; 6 Sid Perks; 7 Gin; 8 Guy Pemberton; 9 Phil Archer; 10 Marjorie Antrobus

32

Welcome to Ambridge: Glebe Cottage

✧ Set in a walled garden near to St Stephen's Church, this picturesque cottage has been in the Archer family for years.

✧ The small two-bedroom property was left to Doris Archer for her lifetime by her employer Letty Lawson-Hope for whom she worked as a kitchen maid and lady's maid.

✧ The house was rented out to a number of Ambridge folk until Doris and Dan bought the freehold and retired there. Their own son Phil and wife Jill would also retire there in 2001.

✧ When Phil and Jill's daughter Shula lived in the cottage, her husband Mark took on the hard task of rethatching the roof.

Farming Festivities

Rural life is not all mucking out and mucking in – there's plenty of festive fun to be had too. Make sure you're not missing out on any of the social highlights in the Ambridge calendar by keeping track of these key annual events.

Apple Day

✧ Takes place every October, on or near the 21st and is usually held at Lower Loxley, on the village green or at one of the farms.

✧ Events and games have included bobbing for apples, apple and spoon races and seeing who can make the longest piece of apple peel.

✧ Apple identification competitions were held in 2001 (where a Pink Lady® tripped up Lynda Snell) and 2005 when tree warden George Barford was stumped by a sneakily placed Borsetshire Beauty.

Village fête

✧ This summertime event takes place between June and August, and has attracted a number of celebrity guests over the years.

✧ While recent fêtes have tended to focus on the more traditional delights of homemade produce stalls and the inevitable beer tent, those of years past have included many more unusual stalls and sideshows and even Miss Ambridge beauty queen competitions. Other past attractions include: a fortune teller (1980), Beautiful Baby competitions won by William Grundy in 1983 and Christopher Carter and Kylie Richards in 1990, a performance by the Edgeley Morris Dancers (1992), Bushtucker Trials (2004), Vegetable Olympics (2006), a town crier competition (2007), Guess the weight of the calf (1979), yourself (1976) and the llama (2003) and even Pet Karaoke (1997).

✧ Walter Gabriel was an avid supporter of the fête throughout the 1960s and introduced a number of his own attractions to the proceedings, such as elephants Rosie and Tiny Tim, performing seals, a hot-air balloon, a steam engine and even a ventriloquist's dummy named Marmaduke.

✧ In 1975 the first prize for the fête's talent competition (donated by Charles Harvey) was a £10 record token.

Ambridge Issues: Agricultural diseases

While agricultural storylines don't always take centre stage on *The Archers*, outbreaks of diseases such as foot-and-mouth and TB have sometimes had catastrophic impacts on the farms and characters on the show, with storylines running for months and in some cases over a year. Cases of foot-and-mouth disease (FMD) occurred on UK farms throughout the twentieth century, and a number of cases were reported in the 1950s, before the major outbreak of 1967. One such case found its way to Brookfield Farm in 1956, when two pigs were reported sick by farmhand Simon. Dan Archer, suspecting the worst, called in the vet who tested the animals. They had the disease and Brookfield was quickly quarantined and PC Bryden stood guard at the gate making sure no one came and went from the farm. As poignant and harrowing as it was listening to Dan and Doris remain on their farm while all their cloven-hoofed beasts were slaughtered, the story was also informative, explaining to the listeners about the possible cause of the outbreak, compensation from the Ministry and the importance of insuring against loss of income. The ten-month story saw Doris Archer considering giving up on farming altogether and the struggles the family faced while they built the farm back up after the cull.

The *Archers* writers made a number of last-minute changes to scripts at the start of 2001 when the largest outbreak of foot-and-mouth disease spread across the UK resulting in two thousand cases of the disease and over ten million sheep and cattle being slaughtered. While none of the Ambridge farms reported cases, the disease found its way to Little Croxley on the other side of Borchester and the effects were felt in Ambridge, with issues of disinfection, isolation and tourism being discussed.

Bovine tuberculosis has caused significant problems for Brookfield Farm. It first reared its head in 1994, when Phil was running the farm, in a storyline that lasted eighteen months. The slow-burning plot accurately illustrated the testing procedures and protocols carried out by vets and officials, the prolonged worry experienced by farmers while they wait for the verdict on their livestock and the stigma attached to a farm after a positive diagnosis. The disease was brought to Brookfield again in 1994 and 1998, and a scare occurred in 2003 after there was a TB outbreak at nearby Bank Farm. More recently, David and Ruth battled an outbreak of Johne's disease in the Brookfield cattle in early 2011, which led to some of the animals being slaughtered.

Family Facts: The Carters

✧ Neil Carter is a church warden and his wife Susan is on the church committee.

✧ Neil failed his tractor proficiency test when he first started working as an apprentice at Brookfield Farm.

✧ Susan Carter (née Horrobin) is the oldest of six children. She has four brothers and a sister.

✧ Susan was sentenced to six months in prison in 1993 for harbouring a fugitive – her brother Clive.

✧ Emma Carter was teased at school when her uncle Clive was involved in the village post office raid.

✧ When he was nine, Christopher Carter trained his hamster to go round its wheel to music for the village fête.

✧ Emma's marriage to Will Grundy was one of the shorter unions in Ambridge's history. They were together for eleven months before she told him she'd rather be with his brother Ed.

✧ Emma started working at Lower Loxley's cafe in 2000, though her current job is as Ruth and David's much-needed cleaner at Brookfield.

Welcome to Ambridge: Glebelands and The Green

✧ This small development of executive homes near to the village green caused quite the Ambridge controversy when landowner Jack Woolley proposed building them in the 1970s.

✧ Laura Archer and Colonel Danby especially made sure the builders stuck rigidly to the plans when they were finally built in 1978 and 1979.

✧ Residents include Derek and Pat Fletcher and Mr and Mrs Patterson.

✧ The Green development opposite the village green has been home to Neil and Susan Carter who bought former council house No. 1 while the Horrobin family have been the long-time disreputable residents at No. 6.

GONE BUT NOT FORGOTTEN:
JOHN 'JACK' ARCHER

Born: 17 December 1922
Died: 12 January 1972

No parents should have to bury their children, so it was truly a sad day for Dan and Doris when Jack Archer died aged just forty-nine years old from liver failure. Their eldest son had lived a somewhat troubled life, despite his marriage to the gregarious Peggy and their three children (Jennifer, Lilian and Tony). He never quite achieved his full potential or truly believed in himself. The farmer's life is a hard one, full of uncompromising choices and physical work, which Jack quickly learned wasn't for him when he had his own Ambridge smallholding. A farming venture in Cornwall also proved unsuccessful when his partner became a little too fond of Peggy, so it was back to Ambridge for the family. The couple soon found themselves behind the bar at The Bull, in 1953.

While Peggy flourished as a natural landlady, Jack felt overshadowed and turned to the drink that was so readily available. A stint in hospital to deal with a nervous breakdown seemed to have helped Jack turn over a new leaf and he was keenly involved with his children – their schooling, their love lives (especially Jennifer's) and their dramas – most memorably when Jennifer found herself pregnant and refused to name the father. While much of his later life was spent using good business sense to buy and renovate the pub thanks to generous donations from his Aunt Laura, Jack couldn't shake off his demons and added gambling to his list of vices. Despite trying to give up drinking, the damage had been done and Jack found himself consigned to a clinic in Scotland battling liver disease. He missed his children's weddings, the births of grandchildren, and being there for wife Peggy through it all.

And the Award goes to...

✧ Script writer and actor Norman Painting (Phil) was awarded the OBE in the New Year's Honours list of 1976. That same year Gwen Berryman (Doris) was voted Midlander of the Year. She went on to receive an MBE at Buckingham Palace in 1981, a year after her character had died.

✧ The programme was awarded the prestigious Sony Radio Gold Award in May 1987.

✧ June Spencer, who plays Peggy Woolley, was made an OBE in 1991.

✧ In 2001, *The Archers'* fiftieth year, Trevor Harrison (Eddie Grundy) was awarded an MBE for his services to radio drama.

✧ At the Variety Club Showbusiness Awards in 2002 Felicity Finch (Ruth Archer) and Tim Bentinck (David Archer) accepted the Radio Personality Award on behalf of the programme.

✧ Graham Seed, who joined the programme as Nigel Pargetter in 1983 and whose character died in the dramatic sixtieth anniversary episode, was awarded Radio Broadcaster of the Year at the 37th Annual Broadcasting Press Guild Awards in 2011.

Quiz Night at The Bull:

Here comes the bride!

1 Which lady wore an apricot-coloured hat to her wedding in 1991?
2 What theme did Jolene Rogers and Sid Perks have for their wedding in 2002?
3 Whose was the first wedding to be heard on the air in 1955?
4 Who gave Polly Mead away at her wedding to Sid Perks because her own father was locked up in the county psychiatric hospital?
5 Who received a second-hand 1952 motor car as a wedding present from his new in-laws?
6 Mrs Ainsley of Churcham made a cream and gold dress for which bride in 1979?
7 Who accompanied Jennifer and Roger Travers-Macy on their post-wedding holiday to Ibiza?
8 Where did Lilian and Ralph Bellamy have their wedding reception?
9 In 1963 Janet Sheldon died four months after marrying which long-time bachelor?
10 Elizabeth Archer and Kate Aldridge were bridesmaids for which couple's nuptials in 1985?

1 Peggy; 2 Country and western; 3 Phil Archer and Grace Fairbrother; 4 Jack Archer; 5 Phil Archer; 6 Christine Archer, on her marriage to George Barford; 7 Adam; 8 Grey Gables; 9 John Tregorran; 10 Shula and Mark's

42

Welcome to Ambridge: Grange Farm

✧ The Grundys used to be tenants here, but they were never afflicted too badly with a work ethic, and this combined with a run of bad luck forced them out of the farm due to bankruptcy in 2000.

✧ When Oliver Sterling first bought 50 acres of Grange Farm he stocked it with beef cattle, before having a change of heart, selling the herd off and replacing them with Guernseys to produce milk.

✧ When TB struck Oliver's herd in 2008 and he almost gave up farming altogether, Ed Grundy offered his services and took over as a tenant farmer.

✧ The Guernsey milk from Grange Farm is also used to make a semi-hard cheese called Sterling Gold, thanks to some help from Helen Archer.

Making *The Archers*: Farming fans and *Archers* addicts

In a time of HD 3D televisual experiences it's comforting to know that *The Archers* remains the world's longest-running drama series – an astounding achievement. With nearly five million listeners tuning in every week in the UK alone the programme is going from strength to strength. *The Archers* is broadcast from Sunday to Friday at 7 p.m. each evening. Each episode is repeated the following day (except on Saturdays – there's no repeat of Friday's episode). If you miss the show during the week you can always catch up with the omnibus edition at 10 a.m. on Sundays or listen to episodes on the BBC iPlayer.

Adapting to the digital climate has been a breeze for the folk of Ambridge: you can download podcasts of the show to listen to on your MP3 player while you plough the fields. *The Archers'* loyal listeners have helped to make it the most popular non-news programme on Radio 4 and the most listened to programme online. The *Archers* production team and actors love to meet the listeners at festivals, book signings and even the launch of Eddie Grundy's CDs. There have even been *Archers* conventions – in 1994 one was held in Malvern, Worcestershire, opened by *EastEnders* actress Wendy Richard. The show's official fan club, Archers Addicts, run by members of the cast, has even held events at Pebble Mill Studios, where the show used to be recorded, so fans could meet the cast and see how the show is put together. Still can't get enough of Ambridge? Past theatre tours of *The Ambridge Pageant* (1991) and *Murder at Ambridge Hall* (1993) saw members of the cast appear in live *Archers* productions and it's now possible to set sail on an *Archers* cruise with some of your favourite characters. Fred. Olsen Cruise Lines give fans the chance to meet the cast, learn about how the programme's sound effects are made and watch a live 'recording' taking place.

Archers listeners are passionate and proactive, and some regularly contribute to a number of unofficial websites discussing characters, storylines and reminiscing over the last sixty years of *Archers* history.

Quiz Night at The Bull:

Doctor, Doctor!

1 Phil Archer was on a business trip in which country when he was hospitalised with an infected foot?

2 In 1958 Pru Forrest spent six months in a sanatorium after being diagnosed with what?

3 Who was admitted to Felpersham Isolation Hospital with diphtheria in 1952?

4 Who did Carol Grey knock off their scooter when she arrived in the village in 1954?

5 Who fell through the ice of the village pond, only to be rescued by her father and Ned Larkin in 1958?

6 Which child was bitten by an adder in 1977?

7 What frozen dish did Freda Fry drop on her foot in 1995?

8 Who infected the entire cast of the 2008 pantomime with flu?

9 What bone did Nigel Pargetter break during his quad bike race with Kenton?

10 Shula was somewhat relieved when son Daniel was diagnosed with systemic juvenile rheumatoid arthritis because she thought he had what illness instead?

Welcome to Ambridge: Grange Spinney

✧ Dubbed the Wisteria Lane of Ambridge, these executive homes lie between the churchyard and Grange Farm.

✧ Grange Spinney residents Sabrina and Richard Thwaite have a large conservatory and a 4x4.

✧ There are twelve luxury homes and six low-cost homes in the development.

✧ Most residents commute to Birmingham for work and shop in Felpersham, not paying much part in the life of the village.

✧ Other residents living in Grange Spinney are the Noakes and their daughter (who goes to boarding school), Barry Simmonds, Mrs Palmer, the Hendricks, the Robinsons, the McWilliamses and the Thompsons.

Family Facts: The Aldridges

✧ Jennifer's early love life included a relationship with Brookfield farmhand Paddy Redmond, which led to the birth of their son Adam, and an unsuccessful first marriage with Debbie's father Roger Travers-Macy, who had previously dated her sister Lilian.

✧ Brian Aldridge is known for his wandering eyes, which have fallen on the likes of Caroline Bone, riding instructor Mandy Beesborough, Siobhan Hathaway and even Betty Tucker (who was wise enough to turn his skinny-dipping offer down) during his marriage to Jennifer.

✧ When he was a child, Adam Macy was bitten by an adder while out riding with friends in Heydon Berrow – he was rushed to hospital and saved by a new anti-venom serum.

✧ Debbie finally ended her relationship with ex-husband and university lecturer Simon Gerrard after walking in on him sharing a passionate kiss with his department head's wife in 2001.

✧ Debbie now lives on a farm in Hungary, and runs Home Farm's arable business by email.

✧ Phoebe Aldridge was born in a tepee at the Glastonbury Festival. Nowadays, her life is a little less unconventional. She attends Borchester Green secondary school and lives with her dad Roy Tucker, step-mum Hayley, and baby sister Abbie.

✧ Alice spent some of her gap year working on an AIDS project in Africa with her sister Kate. More recently, she travelled abroad again – this time to Las Vegas, where she married Chris Carter.

✧ In 2010 Kate Madikane returned to Ambridge to study international development at Felpersham University. Her home is now in Johannesburg with her journalist husband Lucas.

✧ Ruairi Donovan was one of the most controversial additions to the Aldridge clan. The result of an affair between Brian Aldridge and Siobhan Hathaway, Ruairi was brought back to Ambridge by Brian after his mother died of cancer.

Gone but not Forgotten:
Marjorie Antrobus

Born: 1922
Died: 12 August 2008

Married life for Marjorie Antrobus was truly a joy as she travelled the world with husband Teddy on his various army postings. After his death in Nairobi, Marjorie returned to the UK and settled in Borsetshire's Waterley Cross where she bred Afghan hounds – her other true joy in life. One of her hounds even picked up second prize at Crufts. She fell in love with Ambridge after she visited to speak at the Over Sixties Club and moved into Nightingale Farm shortly after. As an Ambridge resident Marjorie got stuck into village life as a bell ringer, acted and sung in village performances, and became an invaluable cricket scorer. She was always closely associated with St Stephen's and supportive of its various vicars, and while she never fell in love again she made some true friends, especially in her lodger Hayley Jordan (now Tucker) who helped her when she developed problems with her sight. After many years of village life, not to mention that surprising blind date with a 'Gentleman farmer seeking companionship' aka Joe Grundy, Marjorie moved into The Laurels retirement home where she passed away.

Welcome to Ambridge: Grey Gables

✧ Ambridge's country house hotel is nestled in 15 acres of gardens.

✧ The four-star hotel was built in the Victorian era in a neo-Gothic style and houses twenty-four en-suite bedrooms. There is also an annexe with a further thirty-six bedrooms.

✧ The Royal Garden Suite is considered to be the best set of rooms in the hotel complex.

✧ In response to the recession chef Ian Craig started serving more affordable bistro fare in addition to the hotel's highly-reputed haute cuisine.

✧ Guests can enjoy a spot of golf at the nearby Ambridge Golf Club, a day of shooting on Home Farm, or an indulgent treat in the Health Club with its indoor pool, gym, sauna and jacuzzi.

✧ The Lodge guards the driveway to Grey Gables and is home to Peggy Woolley – she and husband Jack moved there in 1991.

★ Famous Faces in Ambridge ★

Some more celebrities to grace the humble Ambridge folk with their presence...

✧ **Terry Wogan** made an appearance on the show in 1989 when he popped into Grey Gables to participate in Jack Woolley's celebrity golfing weekend. Wogan's Radio 2 programme also raised £17,000 for Children in Need in 2005 by auctioning off a speaking part in *The Archers* – Wogan appeared as himself again alongside the winning bidder, Christine Hunt, who took on the previously unvoiced character of Grey Gables receptionist Trudy Porter. In the episode, Terry Wogan remembers Trudy participating in a quiz that he hosted.

✧ **Judi Dench** breathed life (and a voice) into Pru Forrest when she appeared alongside Terry Wogan for the show's 10,000th episode in 1989. The quiet character plucked up the courage to give the welcome speech when Terry Wogan arrived at Grey Gables for a celebrity golf tournament.

✧ Although she didn't speak herself, **Esther Rantzen** joined Terry Wogan and Judi Dench in the studio to record the sound effects, including the sound of a telephone being answered, that went along with their 1989 landmark episode.

✧ Radio DJ **John Peel,** himself a life-long fan of *The Archers*, got to fulfil a dream of appearing on the show when in 1991 Radio 1 hosted their annual Christmas dinner at Grey Gables.

✧ When Bond girl **Britt Ekland** took to the stage for Borchester's Christmas pantomime of *Aladdin* in 1992, Eddie Grundy persuaded his boys to enter a colouring competition to see the show and meet her backstage and they won. On true Grundy form, Eddie got a little sloshed on champagne in Britt's dressing room. Some of this episode was recorded at the Birmingham Hippodrome.

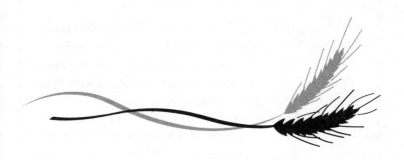

Gone but not Forgotten:
Philip 'Phil' Archer

Born: 23 April 1928
Death: 12 February 2010

Taking the torch from his father Dan Archer, Phil became one of the most respected and trusted patriarchs in Ambridge. His long, loving relationship with wife Jill was a model marriage that lasted for fifty-three years. In the early days of *The Archers* it looked as if nothing could go wrong for young Phil, with his Farm Institute education, as he managed farms for the likes of George Fairbrother and Charles Grenville. The tragic loss of first wife, Grace, in a horrendous fire at Grey Gables could have broken him, but Phil found Jill shortly after, and started life afresh. He soon found himself incredibly busy with their four children – twins Shula and Kenton, followed by singletons David and Elizabeth. Brookfield Farm was Phil's responsibility when his father finally retired and became the focal point for many of the family's dramas – tensions between sons Kenton and David, Shula's disastrous relationships and Elizabeth's heart problems.

Later in life Phil was reminded of the tragic loss of Grace by son-in-law Mark Hebden's death and daughter-in-law Ruth Archer's breast cancer. Through the highs and lows of Ambridge life Phil found joy in music – he played the organ at church and the piano for the Christmas plays – and his dear pigs. Brookfield was hard for Phil to leave, but a chance accident, which left Jill on crutches, found the couple trading places with David and Ruth and temporarily occupying the bungalow. They soon left the farmhouse for good and moved into Glebe Cottage, passing the family business to son David. Phil lived out his final years in the relative peace of Ambridge, finally able to devote time to his passion for astronomy, and to the discovery of the delight of baking, much to Jill's frequent frustration! In early 2010, he was found dead by Jill, sitting in his chair with Elgar's *The Dream of Gerontius* playing in the background.

Quiz Night at The Bull:

Bullseyes, balls and wickets

1 In what year did the cricket pitch move temporarily from the village green to Grey Gables?
2 Who was captain of The Bull's regular darts team in 1989?
3 What two colours did the Ambridge Wanderers football team wear in 1975?
4 Hunting was banned in 2001 because of the outbreak of which disease?
5 Who is the annual Single Wicket Competition played in memory of?
6 Whose cottage was the Ambridge Wanderers' pitch situated behind?
7 Who managed the Ambridge cricket team in 2009?
8 What sport is played to compete for the Viking Trophy?
9 Who was the cricket pavilion named after in 2007?
10 Women were allowed to the cricket club dinner for the first time in 1988 after a petition was organised by which female resident?

1 1983; 2 Neil Carter; 3 Green and white; 4 Foot-and-mouth disease; 5 Mark Hebden; 6 Mrs Perkins's; 7 Sid Perks; 8 Darts; 9 Jack Woolley; 10 Mrs Antrobus

Welcome to Ambridge: Hollowtree

✧ This former farm, once known as Allard's Farm, was bought by Phil Archer in 1962 and was renamed by Phil, Jill and their family when they moved into the farm house.

✧ The house was converted into flats by Nelson Gabriel in the 1970s, but the 'farm' was later bought back by Phil to serve as a home for Brookfield's pigs.

✧ Phil was once heard playing a piano that had been abandoned by Joe and Eddie on the premises.

Family Facts: The Hebdens

✧ Mark Hebden was once the Borchester Under-14 Judo Champion; later in life, he was kicked in the head by a deer he was trying to rescue from a lurcher.

✧ Joanna Hebden's mum put her on a diet when she was two stone overweight to try and help her slim down for Mark and Shula's wedding.

✧ Mark proposed to Shula on Lakey Hill. They returned there after losing their first baby through an ectopic pregnancy and shouted into the wind.

✧ When Bunty Hebden gave daughter-in-law Shula some swan-patterned curtains, Shula said they looked like vultures and gave them to Clarrie Grundy.

✧ On the night Mark died Shula Hebden was hosting Caroline Bone's hen party.

✧ Daniel weighed 7 lb 12 oz when he was born.

Ambridge Issues: Community

Farming may take up a lot of people's time in Ambridge, but social and community issues cause just as much discussion, disagreement and drama. Contentious issues are often drawn from real problems or debates happening around the country and in turn the *Archers'* portrayal of them can have a knock-on effect in other communities. A clear example of this is the storyline involving the community taking over Ambridge's village shop and running it with volunteers to avoid it closing. With village shops seeing a rise in closures over recent years, the programme's writers consulted with The Plunkett Foundation – an organisation that helps communities set up and run a shop – when penning the scripts. With the Ambridge residents having a go at keeping their local amenities alive, and the Foundation being mentioned on the programme, there has been a steady rise in the number of community-run shops since its broadcast. In the past characters have protested and campaigned for schools not to be closed, new housing not to be built and roads not to destroy their countryside. Before his untimely death in 2011, Nigel Pargetter had another wild idea for Lower Loxley to generate income, encourage environmentalism and local produce: allotments. By dedicating some of the estate's ancestral parkland into rentable allotment spaces, Nigel's plan inspired real-life Worcester farmers to turn one of their fields into an allotment space for growing fruit and vegetables.

Flower and Produce Show

Ambridge's gardeners take their green-fingered skills very seriously and each mid-September (although it was held in August in the mid-1980s) they have the opportunity to dazzle the opposition at this judged event in the Village Hall.

The top prizes at the Show are The Lawson-Hope Cup, The Valerie Woolley Memorial Cup and The Nelson Gabriel Memorial Cup for Gentleman's Buttonhole. The Show's overall winner is the competitor who receives the most first prize placements.

Some past overall winners include:

Jean Harvey:	1975, 1977 and 1979 (although she was disqualified in 1979 for using a professional gardener)
Pru Forrest:	1982, 1985 (with a record fifteen prizes), 1991
Freda Fry:	1990
Tom Forrest:	1993
Bert Fry:	1993, 2003

In some years the Flower and Produce Show has been replaced by other events including a flower festival, a ploughing contest and a giant car boot sale.

The Show is not without its village scandal and disagreements. Here are just some from years past:

✧ In 1977 Laura Archer challenged her husband's sister-in-law Doris's first prize lemon curd win, claiming that it was a jar she had given Doris.

✧ Tom Forrest was quite put out in 1994 when young Will Grundy won the best onion category, judged by the French mayor of twinned village Meyruelle – Tom claimed this 'butcher' didn't know what he was talking about.

✧ A burst pipe in the Village Hall caused a mass evacuation during the Show in 2007, which gave Derek Fletcher his chance to switch the name labels on the runner beans so Bert Fry wouldn't win the category. Luckily, Phil Archer switched them back and Bert took the title.

✧ Walter Gabriel accused Pru Forrest of cheating her way to the overall prize winning position in 1982 by using products from the WI in the homemade jams category.

✧ Lynda Snell beat Tom Forrest to first prize in the marrow category in 1995, despite the fact he had given her the seed for her plant.

✧ Pru Forrest neglected to feed husband Tom in her 1985 bid for overall winner – he became the subject of village gossip and snide jaunts from his friends at the pub.

Welcome to Ambridge: Home Farm

✧ The sale of parts of the Bellamy Estate in the 1970s led to the creation of Home Farm.

✧ Home Farm has the largest farmhouse in Ambridge, with a solar-heated swimming pool and luxuriously decorated rooms.

✧ Holiday cottage 'The Rookeries' used to be three farm workers' cottages.

✧ Brian Aldridge diversified the farm in the 1990s when he opened a riding course and a fishing lake on the land.

✧ The 1,585 acre farm is mainly arable with a small lambing flock and deer and is run by Adam Macy and his half-sister Debbie Aldridge.

✧ The farm's maze of maize has been designed in different years as a wizard (The Magi-maze), a spaceship (The Alien Maze) and a dinosaur (The Dino-maze).

✧ Home Farm's tied cottage Casa Nueva has been home to Will Grundy since he returned from his honeymoon in Mexico with now ex-wife Emma – he now lives at this gamekeeper's cottage with Nic Hanson. The name means 'new home' in Spanish.

Fast Facts on Furry Friends

Animals play a huge part in Ambridge life – whether they're being raced, ridden, reared or rounding up the sheep, there's hardly a house in the village that's animal-free. From horses and hounds to llamas and peacocks, Ambridge has been home to a number of memorable creatures over the years.

Dogs

Bessie	John Archer's Labrador–Retriever cross
Bettina	One of Majorie Antrobus's most colourful Afghans
Biff	Working sheepdog at Brookfield Farm
Butch	Walter Gabriel's bulldog was a gift from Debbie Glover; he was put down in 1972
Captain	Jack Woolley's Staffordshire Bull Terrier was famed for eating Susan and Neil Carter's wedding cake
Fly	Working sheepdog at Home Farm
Hermes	Lynda Snell's Afghan puppy
Honey	Hazel Woolley's Bassett Hound was a tenth birthday present but was shot two years later for scaring a flock of sheep
Judy	Tom Forrest's spaniel died in 1961 and was replaced by a Labrador
Meg	Will Grundy's gun dog
Mitch	Formerly Greg Turner's gun dog, now looked after by Will Grundy

Nell	Dan Archer's sheepdog
Portia	Another of Majorie Antrobus's dogs now buried in the garden at Nightingale Farm
Scruff	Daniel Hebden Lloyd's Alsatian cross, now looked after by Lynda because it was too boisterous at The Stables
Timus	Phil Archer was given this corgi by Walter Gabriel and Bill Sawyer after his wife Grace's death
Trigger	Doris Archer's Jack Russell was born in 1964 and lived nearly twelve years
Trouncer	A replacement dog for Hazel Woolley's Honey
Turpin	Jack and Peggy's boxer

Horses

Bartleby	Joe Grundy's pony
Basil	The original Palm Sunday donkey
Benjamin	This donkey, kept at The Stables, took over from Basil for Palm Sunday services
Christina	Paul Johnson's horse that ran at Scowell Bradon
Comet	Helen Archer's hairy, overweight pony, which had to be put down due to laminitis
Grey Silk	Jack Woolley once owned this race horse
Maisie	This horse was given to Caroline by Guy on her fortieth birthday in 1995
Midnight	Grace Archer was trying to save Midnight when she returned to the stable fire that took

	her life; Midnight was Christine Barford's horse
Monarch	Paul Johnson rode this beast at the Heybury Point-to-Point race in 1958
Mister Jones	Olympic showjumper Ann Moore spent part of 1974 training a young Shula Archer on her horse, Mister Jones, believing she had promise
Red Knight	Ralph Bellamy's horse that Lilian rode at the South Borsetshire Point-to-Point; Ralph commissioned a portrait of Lilian on Red Knight
Spearmint	Alice Carter's horse
Tolly	Short for 'Autolycus', this Hanoverian cross thoroughbred was bought for Debbie by Brian Aldridge in 1992
Tootsie	Otherwise known as Hassett Hill Two Timer, shared between Brian Aldridge (75%) and Christine Barford (25%)

Other horses referred to at The Stables include: Marcie, Maxwell, Fleur, Minty, Colfax, Pluto, Sylvester, Nimrod, Silver, Cottonwood, Niobe, Magnet and Duff

Other animals

Eccles	The proud peacock who moved into The Bull in 1993

Barbarella	Known by those that love her as 'Miss Babs', this Berkshire pig belongs to the Grundys
Bill and Ben	Joe Grundy gave these cats to Peggy after the death of her previous feline
Constanza	One of Lynda's llama birthday presents to husband Robert
Demeter	Goat owned by Lynda Snell
Lone Ranger	Freda Fry's stray cat who died from what appeared to be a snake bite in 2007
Persephone	Goat owned by Lynda Snell
Salieri	Constanza and Wolfgang's llama baby
Sammy	Peggy's cat
Wolfgang	Constanza's llama mate

The 1980s Brookfield pig unit at Hollowtree was made up of a lively bunch of boars: Playboy I, II and III, Cromwell, Monty and Hercules

Quiz Night at The Bull:

What's for dinner?

1 What party food did Susan Carter forbid son
   Christopher from eating at the opening of the Dan
   Archer Memorial Children's Playground in 1996?
2 Which Glebe Cottage resident tried and failed
   to make marmalade in 2009 when the jam
   thermometer snapped off in the pan?
3 Name the Birmingham takeaway where Usha Franks
   bought Indian food to feed to the women of the WI?
4 After travelling to India, what was Freda Fry
   inspired to make?
5 Pat Archer was stirring a pan of what when she
   finally broke down after John's death?
6 Who was the unlikely writer of a cookery column
   for the *Borchester Echo*?
7 Mrs Scroby claims adding mustard to beer, boiling
   it and drinking it is a cure for what?
8 What kind of cake competition did Grey Gables
   chef Jean-Paul judge in 1999?
9 Who went on the 'within five miles' diet for Lent in 2009?
10 Whose wedding reception in 1957 featured the
   revolutionary idea of a buffet rather than a
   sit-down meal?

1 Jelly; 2 Phil Archer; 3 Balti Triangle; 4 Chutney; 5 Soup; 6 Elizabeth; 7 Rheumatics; 8
Simnel cake; 9 Pip Archer ; 10 Phil and Jill Archer's

Welcome to Ambridge: Honeysuckle Cottage

- ✧ As one of the most picturesque cottages in Ambridge, thatched Honeysuckle overlooks the duck pond and the village green.

- ✧ Death watch beetle was discovered in the thatch in 1977.

- ✧ A small pile of stones in the garden marks the grave of Nelson Gabriel's daughter's dog Winston.

- ✧ The house was refurbished and extended by previous residents Tim and Siobhan Hathaway.

- ✧ The house is currently occupied by Adam Macy and his civil partner Ian Craig and has its own hot tub.

Gone but not Forgotten:
Tom Forrest

Born: 20 October 1910
Died: 5 November 1998

By the time Tom Forrest was in his forties, his sister Doris Archer and most of his friends had resigned themselves to his bachelor ways. For years he had worked as a gamekeeper, following in the footsteps of his father, William, and found pleasure in the simple things – bell-ringing, singing and the warm welcome he always received at Brookfield Farm. It came as quite a shock then when he took a shine to Bull barmaid Pru Harris after acting as executor of her mother's will; the two struck up a close friendship.

It took the dramatic events of Ned Larkin's brother Bob arriving in Ambridge to bring them closer together. When Bob proposed to Pru, Tom was furious and the two exchanged harsh words. Then when Tom found Bob poaching, there was a tussle, and Bob's gun accidentally went off, killing him. Tom went on trial for manslaughter but was acquitted by the jury – he arrived back in Ambridge to a hero's welcome and the sound of the Hollerton Silver Band playing 'For He's a Jolly Good Fellow'. This trying time led to him proposing to Pru and their wedding in September 1958.

Though they met later in life the couple spent a happy thirty-seven years together, mainly living at Keeper's Cottage built for them by Charles Grenville. They fostered two boys in their time together – Johnny Martin and Peter Stevens – and Tom worked as Sporting Manager for Jack Woolley, and after trying to retire found himself managing Jack's garden centre and fishery. In later life they moved into The Laurels nursing home together. Tom Forrest – the man who loved biscuits, bell-ringing and kept the friendly competition of the Flower and Produce Show alive with his rivalry with Bert Fry – died a week after his beloved wife Pru. Their names are both commemorated on bells in St Stephen's Church tower.

Quiz Night at The Bull:

Love is in the air!

1 Whose wedding were David Archer and Sophie Barlow watching on TV when he proposed to her?

2 Who took Caroline Bone to London for a secret romantic getaway in 1985?

3 Kathy Perks embraced the singles dating scene at a dinner party where she met Richard who was an expert in which piece of office equipment?

4 What kind of ring did David Archer present to his wife Ruth for Christmas in 2000?

5 Name the man who kept his options open in the 1980s by sending Valentine's cards to Shula, Elizabeth and Jill?

6 When her family moved north in 1959 what did Joan Hood give Jimmy Grange as a token of her undying love?

7 Mike Tucker was taken to the theatre by lonely hearts match Wendy. What play did they see?

8 In 1986 a Grey Gables guest from Santa Barbara called Patience Talt was proposed to by which Ambridge resident?

9 When Susan Horrobin won a pig at the village fête in 1983, who offered to build a pen for it and would later became her boyfriend and husband?

10 Who was romanced by handsome wine importer Robin Fairbrother and his BMW?

1 Prince Andrew and Sarah Ferguson; 2 Brian Aldridge; 3 Stapler; 4 An eternity ring; 5 Nigel Pargetter; 6 A bird book; 7 *The Cherry Orchard*; 8 Joe Grundy; 9 Neil Carter; 10 Elizabeth Archer

70

Making *The Archers*: Ambridge has the *Extra*-factor

On 16 March, 2011, the BBC announced that a new programme would air on BBC Radio 4 Extra that April called *Ambridge Extra* – a spin-off show to the long-running *Archers* programme. The digital station would be airing two episodes of the programme on Thursdays at 10 a.m. with repeated episodes at 2.15 p.m. Half-hour omnibus editions would also be aired on Fridays and Sundays. Marking the sixtieth anniversary year of *The Archers*, programme editor Vanessa Whitburn described *Ambridge Extra* as a bonus for listeners who want to spend more time immersed in the lives of the Ambridge characters. While *The Archers* has always been written as a continuous drama with six episodes airing each week, *Ambridge Extra* was planned as a finite series with only two episodes a week, and would therefore only be able to focus on a smaller number of characters and fewer storylines.

Critics of the idea of a spin-off programme slated the BBC for using the carrot of a 'bonus treat' to get dedicated *Archers* fans to make the switch to digital radios so they wouldn't miss out, but the show's makers were keen to dismiss this idea, saying *Archers* fans could still listen to the original programme as a stand-alone series without missing key plot developments. Continuity between the two series would be paramount, but *Ambridge Extra* would take the opportunity to go further afield from Ambridge – with scripts set in Borchester, Southampton and even Las Vegas. And while the production values of the new programme were to be in line with the main show, the pace would be livelier and there would be a stronger focus on the lives of younger characters, such as Alice Carter who is studying at Southampton University.

Welcome to Ambridge: Keeper's Cottage and April Cottage

- ✧ This pair of three-bedroom cottages was built in 1960 by Charles Grenier. They are situated not far from Ambridge Hall.

- ✧ Initially Keeper's Cottage was built to provide accommodation for Charles's workers after the original workers' cottages were demolished to make way for a new road.

- ✧ Former Keeper's Cottage resident, Tom Forrest, helped decide the layout of the house when it was being built and developed the garden into the home for Pru's many prize-winning Flower and Produce Show entries.

- ✧ John Archer moved into April Cottage with Hayley Jordan (now Tucker) in early 1997, and it was where she later caught him cheating on her with ex-love Sharon Richards.

- ✧ Current occupants of April Cottage are Kathy Perks and her son Jamie, while Keeper's Cottage is home to Joe, Eddie and Clarrie Grundy.

Family Facts: The Archers of Bridge Farm

✧ Tony Archer lost his job as a dairy manager for Ralph Bellamy when he skipped work to be with summer school teacher Jane Petrie.

✧ Pat Archer was once the county champion at javelin.

✧ John Archer's favourite childhood storybook was *Little Piggly Wiggly* and the song played by Hayley Jordan (now Tucker) at his funeral was 'Wonderwall' by Oasis.

✧ Helen Archer received six GCSEs and studied for an HND in food technology with management.

✧ Tom Archer's seventeenth birthday was the same day his brother John died.

Welcome to Ambridge: Lower Loxley Hall

✧ Home to the Pargetter family for centuries, stately home Lower Loxley Hall, just two miles east of Ambridge, has Jacobean origins but was added to substantially over time as the year 1702 written over the door indicates.

✧ Most of the house is open to the public for tours and it also doubles up as a conference centre.

✧ Guests can enjoy the toy museum in the old nursery, a treetop walk in the arboretum, a visit to the animals in the rare breeds farm and a high-quality meal from local produce in the Orangery Café.

✧ Lower Loxley Hall is set in 7 acres of picturesque woodland and a further 3 acres of informal gardens. There is a cycle route around the grounds and visitors are able to hire bikes.

✧ Lower Loxley plays host to a number of public events to support the running costs of the property, including December's 'Deck the Halls', which has previously featured a German market and an ice rink and the Easter Egg-Stravaganza in 2006.

✧ Hillside is a two-house development just across the road from Lower Loxley, which was split into flats by property developer Matt Crawford. Friendly milkman Harry Mason was one of the first residents; he was joined shortly afterwards by flatmate-from-hell Jack 'Jazzer' McCreary, but after a few teething problems the two seem to have found a way to coexist peacefully!

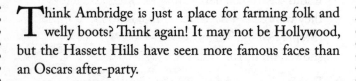

★ Famous Faces in Ambridge ★

Think Ambridge is just a place for farming folk and welly boots? Think again! It may not be Hollywood, but the Hassett Hills have seen more famous faces than an Oscars after-party.

✧ When Lynda Snell needed help getting the Village Hall refurbished in 1993, she called on fundraising challenge legend **Anneka Rice** who arrived in the village ready to get stuck in.

✧ Another self-confessed *Archers* fan found himself on the programme in 2003 when celebrity gardener and TV presenter **Alan Titchmarsh** came to the village to judge Ambridge's entry for the National Garden Scheme.

✧ July 2004 saw celebrated Welsh comedian and presenter **Griff Rhys Jones** attend a reception at Grey Gables. Snared by the persistent Lynda Snell, he soon found himself recruited into her campaign to restore the Cat and Fiddle pub.

✧ While not part of the official programme, comedienne **Victoria Wood**, a dedicated *Archers* fan, wrote a short mini-series for Comic Relief called *Victoria Goes to Ambridge* in 2005 that featured **Stephen Fry, Ewan McGregor, Liza Tarbuck** and **Sir Ian McKellen**. The episodes were aired on

Radio 4 with listeners voting for which celebrity they wanted to take the lead role in the final episode (Stephen won). That same week **Chris Moyles** showed up in The Bull ordering a cocktail.

✧ Fashion icon and designer **Zandra Rhodes** did her bit to promote stylish ways in Borsetshire when she appeared in a September 2006 fashion show episode. She agreed to appear in the programme without hesitation when she was asked, having been a life-long fan of *The Archers* ever since the dramatic episode where Grace Archer died in a barn fire.

Gone but not Forgotten:
Sid Perks

Born: 9 June 1944
Died: 8 June 2010

When Brummie Sid Perks arrived in Ambridge in 1963 fresh out of borstal, he was taken under Jack Woolley's wing and quickly found himself employed as Jack's chauffeur/handyman. He married barmaid Polly who bought and ran the village shop as postmistress, with Sid's help. After experiencing a miscarriage after a raid at the shop, Polly gave birth to a healthy daughter, Lucy. Sid and Polly then sold up the shop and began running The Bull where they set about making dramatic improvements – opening a restaurant, offering bed and breakfast accommodation and restoring the bowling green.

Polly died tragically in a car accident in 1982, leaving Sid distraught and a single father. He married Lucy's form teacher, Kathy Holland (after three proposals) and so began a tumultuous relationship of affairs (Kathy with Dave Barry and Sid with Jolene Rogers) and arguments. They finally became owners of The Bull in 1993 and had a son, Jamie, in 1995, but their responsibilities were not enough to keep them together and Kathy moved out, making way for new vivacious barmaid Jolene, who Sid married in 2002. After eight happy years of marriage to Jolene, Sid died of a heart attack while on holiday in New Zealand visiting daughter Lucy. Both Kathy and Jolene felt the loss very deeply, as did Sid and Kathy's son Jamie.

Quiz Night at The Bull:

Fields and farmers

1 After an outbreak of foot-and-mouth disease in 1956 Dan Archer replaced which breed of cows with Friesians?

2 Which farmer diversified with the introduction of deer and shooting parties in 1987?

3 What business did Mike Tucker start with the compensation money he received after he lost his eye?

4 At which farm was Neil Carter an apprentice?

5 What is the name of the semi-hard cheese Oliver Sterling's Guernsey milk is used to produce?

6 Which estate created Home Farm when parts of it were sold off in the 1970s?

7 What disease was there an outbreak of in Ambridge in 1955?

8 Onto which farm did a German plane crash land during World War Two?

9 In 1951 when Dan Archer bought his first tractor, which of his horses did he sell to Walter Gabriel?

10 The introduction of what in 1984 saw Brookfield reduce its cow herd from 110 to 95?

1 Shorthorns; 2 Brian Aldridge; 3 A market garden; 4 Brookfield Farm; 5 Sterling Gold; 6 Bellamy Estate; 7 Myxomatosis; 8 Grange Farm; 9 Boxer; 10 Milk quotas

Down the Aisle

St Stephen's church has seen its fair share of romantic unions, unfortunately not all of them lasting as long as the starry-eyed young lovers may have initially hoped. Weddings in Ambridge have caused controversy, jealousy and a fair bit of drama, and have been nothing if not memorable. Here is a list of some notable *Archers* weddings, both at the church and elsewhere.

1 January 1991	Peggy Archer and Jack Woolley
1 February 1967	Carol Grenville and John Tregorran
25 February 1984	Susan Horrobin and Neil Carter
1 March 1979	Christine Johnson and George Barford
11 April 1955	Grace Fairbrother and Phil Archer
12 April 2001	Kate Aldridge and Lucas Madikane
24 April 1987	Kathy Holland and Sid Perks
27 August 2004	Emma Carter and Will Grundy
7 May 2001	Hayley Jordan and Roy Tucker
12 May 2000	Debbie Aldridge and Simon Gerrard
26 May 1969	Lilian Archer and Lester Nicholson
26 May 2005	Julia Pargetter and Lewis Carmichael
29 May 1976	Jennifer Travers-Macy and Brian Aldridge
30 May 1994	Lucy Perks and Duncan Gemmell
25 June 1972	Betty and Mike Tucker
29 June 1963	Janet Sheldon and John Tregorran
29 June 2006	Caroline Pemberton and Oliver Sterling
4 July 2002	Jolene Rogers and Sid Perks
15 July 2009	Vicky Hudson and Mike Tucker

28 July 2010	Alice Aldridge and Christopher Carter
27 & 29 August 2007	Usha Gupta and Alan Franks (they had a Hindu ceremony followed by a Christian ceremony two days later)
3 September 1971	Lilian Nicholson and Ralph Bellamy
11 September 1995	Caroline Bone and Guy Pemberton
21 September 1985	Shula Archer and Mark Hebden
27 September 1966	Polly Mead and Sid Perks
27 September 1968	Jennifer Archer and Roger Travers-Macy
29 September 1994	Elizabeth Archer and Nigel Pargetter
4 October 2006	Eileen Pugsley and Edgar Titcombe
16 November 1957	Jill Patterson and Phil Archer
21 November 1981	Clarrie Larkin and Eddie Grundy
12 December 1974	Pat Lewis and Tony Archer
14 December 2006	Adam Macy and Ian Craig (civil partnership)
15 December 1988	Ruth Pritchard and David Archer
17 December 1921	Doris Forrest and Dan Archer
24 December 1999	Shula Hebden and Alistair Lloyd

GONE BUT NOT FORGOTTEN:
JOHN ARCHER

Born: 31 December 1975
Died: 25 February 1998

While many tragedies have fallen on the folk of Ambridge over the years, for Pat and Tony Archer the loss of their eldest son, John, in 1998 was probably their darkest hour. At just twenty-two years old, things were just getting going for the ambitious youngster who had undertaken a National Diploma in Agriculture at Borchester College and raised his own fully organic pigs. A rebellious older child by nature, John had got off to a rocky start, with only a mild interest in farming. His attentions were more often shared between American football and girls. When teen mum Sharon Richards moved into the caravan at Bridge Farm, his parents thought his infatuation unhealthy and were relieved to pack him off to an agricultural school in Somerset. But his feelings for Sharon didn't abate, and later during his gap year, after a row with his mother about Sharon not taking responsibility for damaging Peggy's van, he stormed out to live with Sharon in her council house. When Sharon left John and Ambridge for Leeds, he was heartbroken and turned to a string of girls to help him move on. Last in line was Hayley Jordan (now Tucker) who he met at a Birmingham nightclub. Just when things were looking good for John – he was living with Hayley at April Cottage, working for his dad and raising his pigs – Sharon arrived back on the scene and he began an affair with his former girlfriend. Caught red-handed by Hayley, it took her leaving for John to realise that he had made a big mistake. When a wedding proposal at the expensive Mont Blanc restaurant wasn't enough to win her back, John was heartbroken. The next day, on his brother's seventeenth birthday, he headed out in the cabless vintage Ferguson tractor to repair a fence and never came back. His lifeless body was found trapped beneath the tractor by his father Tony.

Welcome to Ambridge: Nightingale Farm

✦ Nightingale Farm once belonged to Lady Isabel Lander – the wealthy heiress had inherited it from her uncle Brigadier Winstanley.

✦ When Hugo Barnaby bought the house from Isabel he used most of the building as a youth club and arts and crafts centre.

✦ Neil and Susan Carter rented the property from Hugo as their first home together. Later he offered them £4,000 to leave the flat so he could sell it, which they did and moved to No. 1 The Green.

✦ Nightingale Farm is only a farm by name but was home to Marjorie Antrobus's eight Afghan hounds when she was the owner.

✦ Currently owned by Matt Crawford, the house has seen a number of tenants including Ruth Archer and Nigel Pargetter, Richard Locke and Hayley and Roy Tucker, all of whom took their turn as Marjorie's lodgers over the years.

Quiz Night at The Bull:

Farming fashions

1. After seeing Julia Pargetter on stage in the 1940s and handing her a rose, what gift did her future husband Gerald send to her?
2. Which two women set up a rather unsuccessful fashion business together in the 1980s?
3. Who used to dazzle audiences in fringed and rhinestone-decorated buckskin shirts in his country and western days?
4. Which popular item of clothing does Lynda never wear?
5. Whose party trick used be undoing girls' bras through their clothes?
6. Who presented Shula with a grass skirt when he returned home on leave from the Merchant Navy in 1975?
7. In 1998 Peggy organised a fashion show at Grey Gables. Which store provided the clothes?
8. What item of clothing did Marjorie give to Joe Grundy when he tried lonely hearts dating in the late 1980s?
9. What woolly item did Martha Woodford knit for all the village children?
10. What colour Bo Peep-style dresses did Elizabeth Archer's bridesmaids wear to her wedding to Nigel Pargetter?

1 A fox-fur coat; 2 Elizabeth Pargetter and Sophie Barlow; 3 Eddie Grundy; 4 Jeans; 5 Nigel Pargetter; 6 Kenton Archer; 7 Underwoods; 8 A Harris tweed jacket; 9 Hats; 10 Pink

84

Family Facts: The Snells

✧ Robert is a keen cricketer and was snapped up by the village team when they heard he was a member of the MCC.

✧ Lynda's slogan for her 1987 Ambridge Parish Council election campaign was 'Snell for a greener Ambridge'. She continues to fill this important civic role in the village, along with her unofficial role as general busybody.

✧ Robert's first wife and the mother of his daughters, Leonie and Coriander, is called Bobo.

✧ Lynda once used the nom de plume Dylan Nells when writing for *Borsetshire Life* magazine.

✧ Robert is a computer software specialist by trade, though since being made redundant he has reinvented himself as Ambridge's 'Mr Fix-It'.

✧ Unable to have children of her own, Lynda has been the 'mother' of a number of animals in her time: goats, puppies, hedgehogs and even ladybirds.

✧ Coriander has her own son called Oscar who step-grandma Lynda adores.

✧ Leonie visited Ambridge early in 2011 at the same time as Lilian's son James; Lynda and Robert were delighted to discover that the two had become an item.

Making *The Archers*: Dissecting 'Dum-di-dum'

Even for those people who claim never to have listened to *The Archers*, or even Radio 4, the 'dum-di-dum' opening melody to the programme is widely recognised. The piece of music itself is actually entitled 'Barwick Green' and is a maypole dance from the 1924 suite *My Native Heath* by Yorkshire composer Sir Arthur Wood. The title refers to a village east of Leeds called Barwick-in-Elmet. Sidney Torch conducted the original orchestral recording used to introduce and close the programme from 1950; the theme was re-recorded in stereo in 1992 and an alternative version has also been recorded by Somerset folk band The Yetties for the Sunday omnibus edition of the programme. It's hard to imagine *The Archers* without that memorable tune, but on April Fool's Day in 2004 the Today programme ran a story revealing that the theme tune was being updated by ambient music composer Brian Eno. In a very convincing interview, Eno stated that there was only so much 'dum-di-dum' anyone could take in a lifetime, and that *The Archers* wanted to move with the rest of the world into the twenty-first century. Needless to say, the original theme tune has remained and isn't going anywhere any time soon. In 2011, as part of Radio 3's Light Fantastic festival, amateur musicians were invited to download their instrument's part for 'Barwick Green' and upload a video of them performing it. The resulting performances were mixed to create an online orchestra performance to be broadcast on Radio 3. So well-loved and embedded in popular culture is the tune that comedian Billy Connolly once suggested it replace 'God Save the Queen' as the British national anthem. And when folk band Bellowhead re-recorded the tune for *Archers* spin-off programme *Ambridge Extra*, the change was met with scepticism by most fans. The *Guardian* described the new version as sounding like a 'French-themed booze-up on Captain Pugwash's pirate ship'. Sir Arthur is probably turning in his grave.

Welcome to Ambridge: Rickyard Cottage

✧ This tiny cottage behind the rick yard on Brookfield Farm was described by herdsman Graham Collard as too small to swing a cat.

✧ Once a workers' cottage, it has been the home of Simon and Bess Cooper, Ned and Mabel Larkin and Tony Archer in the 1970s.

✧ It was reverted into a home for Brookfield Farm workers – Mike Tucker lived there, followed by Graham Collard and his wife Val who both moved out in 1991.

✧ Lisa and Craig found the cottage the ideal place to squat in 1992; it was later turned to profitable use as a holiday let.

✧ Rickyard is now home to Ed and Emma Grundy, Emma's son George and their new baby, Keira.

Quiz Night at The Bull:

Out of town

1. At which station did Phil Archer propose to Jill Patterson?
2. In which Borsetshire village is The Half Moon pub?
3. What does Bentham's in Borchester sell?
4. Where was the salsa club that Ruth Archer and Usha Gupta (now Franks) attended?
5. What's the posh restaurant called in Waterley Cross?
6. There used to be a business in Borchester called Sidney's – what was it?
7. What kind of food does Borchester's El Dorado bar/restaurant serve?
8. What is Penny Hassett's Sundial House?
9. Borchester is twinned with a town in which country?
10. How many miles is Ambridge from Felpersham?

Gone but not Forgotten:
Martha Woodford

Born: 31 July 1922
Died: 17 January 1996

Thank goodness for Martha Woodford working at the village shop – without her Ambridge's residents would never have kept on top of all the gossip and goings-on in the village. This Penny Hassett lass had once been married to postman Herbert Lily and arrived in the village as a widow in 1970 to work part-time in the Ambridge Hall field studies centre. Not shy of getting her hands dirty she took on cleaning work for Doris Archer and scrubbed away at The Bull. Perhaps tiring of doing other people's dirty work, Martha's life took a new turn in 1972 when she married forestry expert Joby Woodford and approached Jack Woolley about working in the village shop. After an initial refusal, and a brief post at Ralph Bellamy's garage, she began working for Jack and took over from Angela Cooper as manager. She introduced an off-licence section and home delivery service and even considered buying the shop when Jack briefly put it on the market.

Martha's marriage to Joby, and their life together at April Cottage, were relatively happy. And even though it was too late for them to start a family, they opened their home up to farming apprentice Neil Carter who they came to regard as a son. After Joby's death in 1993 Martha remained single, although she did take full advantage of the attentions of Joe Grundy and Bill Insley, by getting them to fix her garden gate and chop her firewood. She left her managerial role at the shop in 1989 and stayed on part-time, supporting new boss Betty Tucker through the ordeal of an armed raid in 1993. In January 1996 the little birds of Ambridge must have not known who to turn to with their twitterings of gossip when Bert Fry found Martha dead in her garden holding a bunch of snowdrops in her hand.

Welcome to Ambridge: River Am

✦ Ambridge gets its name from the River Am, which runs through the idyllic Am Vale to Borchester.

✦ Philologists believe the river was originally named the Ambra – this pre-Saxon Celtic word means 'water'.

✦ Other waterways in Borsetshire include the River Mercer, the River Perch and the Felpersham Canal.

✦ Properties located near the river include Ambridge Hall, Brookfield Bungalow, Nightingale Farm, Glebelands and the Vicarage.

Farmer Drama

The Archers may be an everyday story of country folk, but that doesn't mean Ambridge is free from the drama, disaster and freak farming accidents that happen in the real world. In more than sixty years and over 16,000 episodes those good country folk have been witness to and part of all kinds of drama.

1955
When ITV launched as a brand new channel (a commercial rival to BBC broadcasting) on 22 September, they were faced with tough competition from *The Archers* when Grace Archer – Phil's pretty new bride – found herself trapped in a burning stable and died. In 2008 the BBC released confidential documents that revealed Grace's death was a deliberate move by the BBC to steal viewers from ITV and that it had worked. Grace's death made the front page of the papers and was broadcast to eight million listeners.

1957
Hearing Tom Forrest's struggle with poacher Bob Larkin as the two scrambled about before a shotgun went off was the power of radio drama at its best. Who fired the gun? Who was hurt? Luckily, Tom Forrest survived the fight, the shooting and the ensuing manslaughter trial that followed. But the intervening period was fraught with tension, poignancy and some truly tear-jerking scenes.

1963
Those Borsetshire country roads are no stranger to traffic accidents, but this one was pretty horrific. After John Tregorran finally moved on from his feelings for Carol Grenville and married Janet, she was taken from him four months later when Carol's husband Charles Grenville gave her a lift and they were involved in a serious car accident. Charles lost his leg, but Janet lost her life.

1969

Polly Perks had a miscarriage after a shocking raid on the village post office where she worked.

1972

When an RAF plane crashed in the local area, the whole village helped to hunt for survivors.

1974

Tom and Pru Forrest found George Barford semi-conscious after he had attempted to kill himself by taking an overdose of sleeping pills. Luckily, he survived and soon found himself living with Nora McAuley who moved in to take care of him.

1982

Those dreaded rural roads caused havoc once again when Polly Perks's life came to an abrupt end. Driving to the cash and carry with Pat Archer, the car skidded on a bend in the road and hit a milk tanker sideways on, killing Polly instantly.

1989

While campaigning to be a local councillor, Brian Aldridge was canvassing the Grundys when he pushed Joe out of the way of a cow suffering with BSE, subsequently being kicked in the head himself. After an operation to remove a blood clot and cerebral abscess he suffered from post-traumatic epilepsy.

1992

The effects of Elizabeth Archer's abortion were felt throughout her family. After boyfriend Cameron Fraser disappeared from Ambridge, Elizabeth was left devastated and pregnant and despite her mother's protests went through with an abortion. Shula was distressed to discover what her sister had done, as she and husband Mark had been unsuccessfully trying for a baby themselves.

1993

An armed raid on the village shop saw Betty, Debbie, Jack and Kate held hostage by Clive Horrobin and his friend Bruno Wills.

2000

When Ruth Archer found a lump in her breast which turned out to be malignant she underwent a mastectomy and a punishing course of chemotherapy to beat the disease. Listeners were privy to Ruth's fear of leaving her children motherless and her struggle to be intimate with David after the ordeal.

2004

After befriending the quiet chef Owen King during the village production of *A Christmas Carol* Kathy Perks was left shattered after he attacked and raped her and then acted as if nothing had happened. When she finally told ex-husband Sid what had happened he scared Owen into leaving Ambridge for good. She did not go to the police until 2007 after learning Owen had attacked another woman.

2010

Her family may not have approved, but that didn't stop Helen Archer going ahead with her sperm-donor pregnancy. With mum Pat's full support she gave birth to Henry Archer on 2 January 2011.

2011

Nigel Pargetter took to the roof of Lower Loxley to remove a New Year's banner, despite icy conditions. He ended up falling from the roof to his death while David Archer watched helplessly. This storyline was part of *The Archers* sixtieth anniversary episode and was widely discussed in the media in the build-up and aftermath.

Quiz Night at The Bull:

1 Where did John Tregorran travel to in 1964 to get over the death of his wife Janet?
2 Which of Sid Perks's wives got to go to Nashville for their honeymoon?
3 Which European destination did Jack and Peggy head to in May 1966?
4 Who almost travelled to Ethiopia in the 1950s with the eccentric Lady Hylberow?
5 What crime occurred at Brookfield while Dan and Doris Archer were holidaying in Ireland?
6 Which couple headed to Bali for their honeymoon?
7 When Jennifer and Brian Aldridge became frustrated with the delays to the Home Farm swimming pool, where did they jet off to?
8 Who took their children to the Isle of Man for a holiday in 1968?
9 What did Phil Archer shrink in the wash while Jill was on holiday in Sidmouth?
10 Who embarked on a sailing holiday in 1958?

1 Spain; 2 Jolene Perks; 3 The Italian Riviera; 4 Christine Archer; 5 Burglary; 6 Nigel and Elizabeth Pargetter; 7 The Seychelles; 8 Phil and Jill Archer; 9 Her cashmere cardigan; 10 Carol Grey

Welcome to Ambridge: St Stephen's Church

✧ St Stephen's is built on the site of an early seventh-century Augustinian church.

✧ The church tower is 56 feet high and leans 6 inches to the west.

✧ The font is decorated with carved human heads and flowers and is thought to be a gift to the church from Edward I.

✧ A plaque in the church commemorates a peal rung in 1896 that lasted for three hours and twenty minutes.

✧ There is a window in the church dedicated to the memory of Grace Archer.

✧ In 1992 building working for a ramp and toilet revealed ancient timbers which were removed for carbon dating.

✧ The church has attracted its fair share of wildlife over the years including flittermice bats in 1976, a swarm of bees who set up camp near one of the bells and mice who ate their way through the organ stops. The current occupants are a peregrine family that nest in the tower.

Family Facts: The Frys

✧ Bert and Freda have a son called Trevor who is married to Barbara. Trevor and Barbara have a daughter called Amy who Bert doted on as a child.

✧ Bert Fry had his fifteen minutes in the spotlight after Elizabeth Archer wrote about his poetic skills in the *Borchester Echo*. He was even asked to be on regional television programme *In Your Corner* to show off his talent.

✧ Bert was strongly opposed to having a woman vicar at St Stephens's when Janet Fisher first arrived.

✧ Freda played the fairy in the 1998 village production of *Jack and the Beanstalk*.

✧ Having retired from his work as a farmhand at Brookfield, Bert now conducts guided tours at Lower Loxley and is a keen cricket umpire.

✧ Freda is well known in Ambridge and the surrounding area for dishing up traditional English pub grub at The Bull.

GONE BUT NOT FORGOTTEN:
GRACE ARCHER

Born: 2 April 1929
Died: 22 September 1955

Although Grace spent only a few years on the programme, her death remains one of *The Archers'* most talked-about storylines. Grace Fairbrother, the spoilt, beautiful and somewhat coquettish only child of George Fairbrother, caught the attention of Phil Archer straight away. From her arrival in Ambridge she got stuck in with the social scene, promoting the tennis club and becoming secretary of the Young Farmers. Before Grace found herself standing at the altar with Phil she dallied with the likes of Korean War veteran Alan Carey and the Squire's nephew Clive Lawson-Hope, both of whom proposed, but she got jealous when Phil started dating chicken keeper Jane Maxwell. She even went so far as to find Jane a suitable replacement for Phil, just to stop them becoming more serious. Grace's money and position were a concern to Phil, who eventually proposed but insisted on making money through a pig-breeding scheme before they wed. Tired of waiting, and unsuited to the farming lifestyle, Grace left for Ireland and a year of equestrian training. On her return she was cornered by Phil and agreed to marry him; the couple finally tied the knot on Easter Monday of 1955.

Signs of incompatibility were beginning to show early on when Grace expressed a desire to wait before they had children, while Phil was keen to start a family right away. But the future of the couple was cruelly cut short when a stable fire at Grey Gables claimed Grace's life. She had returned to the burning barn to save Christine Barford's horse and became trapped under a fallen beam. She died in Phil's arms on the way to the hospital, leaving listeners shocked and saddened and the future of the Archer family uncertain.

Village Productions (Act I)

Ambridge may not be the East End of London or a particularly dangerous terraced street in Manchester, but it still has its fair share of drama. Of course, nowhere do the villagers revel in the delights of dramatic expression as much as in the amateur productions put on in the Village Hall. Here are details of just some of these theatrical memories.

❖ 1991 *Aladdin* and *Aladdin* – Lynda Snell's script for *Aladdin*, which she had staged in Sunningdale a few years before arriving in Ambridge, was rejected by the Village Hall Committee in favour of Bert Fry's for being outdated. Disheartened but not defeated Lynda decided to go ahead with her own version on the same night at Ambridge Hall. The two plays went head-to-head with Eddie Grundy playing the role of Wishee Washee in both productions, without the directors' knowledge. He was driven to and fro between scenes without them even knowing.

❖ 1996 *Cinderella* – Larry Lovell's production of this fairy-tale classic included Lynda Snell as a resentful Fairy Godmother and Larry himself as Baron Hardup. When Lynda was delayed arriving to one performance, Larry decided to perform both roles by himself. The audience definitely got their money's worth when Lynda showed up and both Fairy Godmothers appeared on stage together.

- ✧ 1997 *A Midsummer Night's Dream* – This open-air production, directed by Lynda Snell, was held in the grounds of Lower Loxley. Lynda put aside her competitive feelings towards fellow thespian Larry Lovell and cast him as Theseus – his preferred role was Lysander, but Lynda decided he was too old for the part.

- ✧ 1999 *Babes in the Millennium Wood* – Lynda Snell was particularly hurt when Larry Lovell went out of his way to insult her production in his review of this show in the *Borchester Echo*. The review focused on the smell of pig manure rather than commenting on the actors or the direction. His one compliment was reserved for the costumes, put together by Jill Archer.

- ✧ 2000 *Mikado* – The show must go on and this one in particular was a great success; but for a while there it looked unlikely that Lynda Snell's production of this W. S. Gilbert comic opera would make it to performance night. Lynda had to deal with Tom Archer's complicated love life causing cast members to quit and Christine Barford putting her back out at the dress rehearsal. Not to mention the real costume drama when the hire company botched their order and sent them the Felpersham Light Opera Society's costumes for Venetian opera *The Gondoliers* instead.

- ✧ 2003 *The Ambridge Mystery Plays* – With the arrival of new vicar Alan Franks a decision was made to give the Christmas production more of a religious theme. This was a peripatetic production that took place at St Stephen's Church, the village green and Brookfield Farm. It starred Susan Carter as Mary and Kenton Archer as her Joseph.

Quiz Night at The Bull:

New life, new strife

1 Which of Clarrie Grundy's sons was two weeks overdue?

2 Before Christine and Paul Johnson adopted Peter, they almost adopted a baby from which country?

3 Who gave birth to her first baby in a tent at the Glastonbury Festival?

4 Coriander Snell was conceived after her parents ate a particularly good meal – but what kind of cuisine was it?

5 Who gave Ruairi Donovan their grandfather's fob watch as a christening present?

6 What condition did Emma Carter have when she was born in 1994?

7 Who left a cricket match against Edgeley two runs short of a half-century in 1997 to make it to the birth of his son?

8 Helen Archer was born breech and with a dislocation of which joint?

9 Who was born with a cleft lip and palate in 1988?

10 Which Archer was born in Australia at 6.20 a.m. on Friday 11 May 2001?

1 William; 2 France; 3 Kate Aldridge; 4 Indian; 5 Brian Aldridge; 6 Jaundice; 7 David Archer; 8 Hip; 9 Christopher Carter; 10 Meriel

100

Welcome to Ambridge: The Bull

✧ The Bull is a black-and-white half-timbered building residing near the village green. Traditional Shires ale is served alongside home-cooked food.

✧ Jack and Peggy Archer paid £5,300 for The Bull when they bought it in 1959.

✧ Sid and Polly Perks took over as landlords of the pub in 1972, but it wasn't until 1993 that Sid owned the property, buying it from Peggy for £250,000 with the help of investment from Guy Pemberton.

✧ In 1995 Kathy Perks revamped The Bull's restaurant with a Civil War theme. On the menu were syllabub, humble pie and Cromwell pudding.

✧ Landlady Jolene Perks has had a number of money-spinning ideas for the pub including: the cyber-café, a midweek carvery and using the function room as 'The Bull Upstairs' for special music nights.

✧ There are two bars – the public bar and the slightly more upmarket Ploughman's bar.

✧ There is a pet peacock called Eccles who lives in the beer garden.

Some famous faces to feature on the programme have put their voices to other characters rather than playing themselves and some haven't said anything at all...

✦ When Sid and Jolene Perks were at Lords Cricket Ground for the npower Village Cup final in 2007 Sid went missing for an hour. When Jolene finally spotted him being led towards an MCC box by none other than former England cricket captain **Mike Gatting**, the anxious landlady gave chase to save her husband from his 'kidnapper'.

✦ As one of Britain's leading medical academics, heralded for his research into human fertility, **Professor Robert Winston (Lord Winston)** was more than happy to feature in an *Archers* storyline in his effort to popularise science. In 2007 he played Roy and Hayley Tucker's medical consultant on the programme, who tried to investigate why the couple were having trouble conceiving.

✦ In 2009, Turner Prize-winning sculptor **Anthony Gormley's** Trafalgar Square project 'One & Other' invited members of the public to apply to stand on a plinth for one-hour time slots over one hundred days. After all the Ambridge residents' applications were rejected, Phil suggested Lynda create an Ambridge plinth for the village fête. Gormley was invited to Ambridge to open the fête and judge the participants – a photographic book of his sculptures was the prize for the winner, Molly Button.

- ✧ Lynda Snell's Whodunnit? theme for the 2010 village fête set fans' tongues wagging about which famous mystery writer would be invited to Ambridge to open the event. Fittingly, *Archers* fan **Colin Dexter** was chosen and presented the prize for solving the murder mystery. *Archers* editor Vanessa Whitburn saw inviting the author as a great chance to repay the favour for his character Inspector Morse's dedication to *The Archers* in his books.

- ✧ No recent celebrity appearance on the programme has been more talked about than that of **Camilla, Duchess of Cornwall's** in 2011. Recorded at Clarence House to mark the twenty-fifth anniversary of the National Osteoporosis Society and the sixtieth anniversary of *The Archers*, the Duchess played herself sipping tea and eating biscuits at a charity function at Grey Gables. She even complimented chef Ian Craig on his shortbread.

Ambridge Issues: Homophobia

You can't please everyone all of the time, but on the whole Ambridge residents are an amiable bunch. Unlike other serial dramas, which have seen gay characters suffer painful bullying, violence and prejudice, the programme's first gay couple – Adam Macy and Ian Craig – didn't face many problems from most of the village's conservative set. Compared to some heterosexual relationships and affairs in Ambridge which have caused no end of debate and controversy, Adam and Ian, who shared their first kiss in a strawberry field in April 2004, had instead to face Sid Perks's homophobia, Ian's coming out to his conservative Protestant family, Adam's step-father Brian Aldridge's objections to the civil partnership, and Adam's grandmother Peggy feeling uncomfortable with their relationship. The couple made history when they had Ambridge's first civil partnership ceremony in 2006 – a year after the UK's first civil partnerships. The episode attracted an extra 250,000 listeners to the programme and was praised by the gay media for its more rounded and thoughtful portrayal of a homosexual relationship. The episode made history by being the first serial drama to feature a gay civil ceremony.

Welcome to Ambridge: The Dower House

✧ This fine country house with slate roof and large garden was the residence of Berrow Estate owners Ralph and Lilian Bellamy between 1970 and 1975.

✧ The egregious Cameron Fraser lived here in the 1990s and renovated in a flashy style, which didn't go down well with future residents Guy and Caroline Pemberton.

✧ Will Grundy lived in the Dower House's self-contained flat after his family were evicted from Grange Farm in 1999.

✧ Self-made businessman Matt Crawford moved into The Dower House with its former mistress, Lilian Bellamy. It's now the base for their latest venture, Amside Property Developments.

Quiz Night at The Bull:

Competitions, curtseys and curtain-ups

1. What event took place instead of the Flower and Produce Show in 1989?
2. What wartime-themed team name did Kathy Perks and Hayley Tucker give themselves in the fête in 2005?
3. Which Borchester pub renamed itself The Old Corn Mill?
4. Who donated the pig for the barbeque held on the day of Prince Charles and Lady Diana Spencer's wedding?
5. Susan Carter wore the 1998's Easter Bonnet Competition winning bonnet, but who had made the hat?
6. What song helped the Ambridge WI reach the regional finals of a choral competition in 1969?
7. Who was awarded the prize for Longest Runner Bean in the Children's Section at the 1999 Flower and Produce Show?
8. What did Kenton Archer spill on one of Lower Loxley's antique silk carpets during his game of 'Murder'?
9. Which couple donated three ballroom dancing lessons to a 2004 auction to raise money for homeless people in Columbia?
10. Alice Aldridge played the part of Snow White in the 2006 Christmas production, but who played her prince?

1 Giant car boot sale; 2 Mums' Army; 3 The Dirty Duck; 4 Phil Archer; 5 Christopher Carter; 6 'The Brilliant and The Dark'; 7 Pip Archer; 8 Fake blood; 9 Mike and Betty Tucker; 10 Fallon Rogers

106

Welcome to Ambridge: The Stables

✧ Situated opposite Bull Farm House, The Stables has been home to Shula Hebden Lloyd since 2001 when she moved in with husband Alistair and son Daniel.

✧ The buildings stand on what was originally known as Sixpenny Farm and then Barratt's farm before being sold to Laura Archer in 1965.

✧ The Stables is also a full-time livery business for Shula and includes a riding school and indoor riding arena. It also houses Alistair's veterinary practice.

✧ The property's previous name was Onemomona, a Maori word meaning 'home, sweet home', named by Laura Archer in recognition of her New Zealand connections.

Oh, So Quiet!

Ssshhh!!

While some Ambridge folk never know when to keep their mouths shut, others are a little less upfront. *The Archers* gives listeners a glimpse at the different goings on in the village but never lets us hear everyone or everything, meaning some characters, while being referred to and acknowledged for years on the programme might never find their voice on the airwaves. Here are some of Ambridge's most silent residents.

✧ **Baggy** – Eddie Grundy's friend helped him create a corn circle, lived on Grange farm with his partner Sylvia and six children in a bus and a tepee and played the rear end of a cow in the 1998 village production of *Jack and the Beanstalk*.

✧ **Fat Paul** – Another of Eddie Grundy's friends, Fat Paul is heavily tattooed and once put Eddie in touch with loan shark Mike Butcher. Eddie persuaded him to join in the tug-of-war fundraiser for the pub team in 2004, as a counterweight to Ronnie the farrier on the church's team, but despite his size he wasn't a great help and the pub lost.

Ssshhh!!

✧ **Mandy Beesborough** – This red-headed gal ran the pony club in 1987 and caught Brian Aldridge's attention – he even invited her to join his party at the horse races on the day his daughter Alice was being born. Some village voices say that nowadays the glorious red of her hair comes [whisper it] *from a bottle…*

✧ **Reg Hebden** – Mark and Joanna's father was a solicitor until he retired. He is married to Bunty and together they insisted their grandson Daniel didn't go to state school.

- **Rhys Evans** – The Welsh barman at The Bull, who was finally given a voice in *Ambridge Extra.*

- **Neville Booth** – Enthusiastic bell-ringer Neville joined the St Stephen's team in 1998 but his car was stolen while he was at practice. He has a nephew called Nathan (also a man of very few words).

- **Derek Fletcher** – Married to Pat, chatty Derek moved into Glebelands in 1983 and visited Meyruelle in France as part of the village-twinning process. He often complains about backache and has a collection of garden gnomes in his garden.

Ssshhh!!

- **Pru Forrest** – Originally voiced by Mary Dalley, the Bull barmaid who married Tom Forrest disappeared into silent-ville in the 1970s and 1980s, despite being involved in a number of important storylines. She worked as a housekeeper at Brookfield Farm and became a determined entrant in the annual Flower and Produce Show. She famously spoke up (played by Judi Dench) and gave the welcoming speech to Terry Wogan when he came to Ambridge in 1989.

- **Freda Fry** – Bert's wife Freda is famed for her cooking; her pies in particular are a local speciality at The Bull. A quiet lady by nature, she spends lots of her time in her own kitchen preparing jams and pickles for the Flower and Produce Show.

- **John Higgs** – Jack Woolley's chauffeur and handyman is a keen gardener and long-term smoker who came to Grey Gables in 1966.

- **Shane** – The good-looking, smart and sensitive chef at Nelson's wine bar was renowned for his cheesecake and worked for Nelson Gabriel for over ten years. He even made his special quiche for his former boss's wake.

✧ **Trudy Porter** – Faithful Trudy first appeared in 1984 working as a waitress at Grey Gables, and slowly rose through the ranks, becoming an assistant manager and receptionist. She once had thespian aspirations and auditioned for a part in one of Lynda Snell's plays. After over thirty years of service she handed in her resignation, speaking for the first time as she did so.

Ssshhh!!

✧ **Eileen Titcombe (previously Pugsley)** – Mrs Titcombe (widow of the late Mr Pugsley) is the housekeeper at Lower Loxley Hall whose first name wasn't revealed until she married Edgar Titcombe in 2010.

✧ **Edgar Titcombe** – Known by everyone as Titcombe, Lower Loxley's head gardener has always gone above and beyond his job description, taking care of the Pargetters' peacocks, and developing nature trails and a treetop walk in the grounds. He is now married to housekeeper Eileen.

✧ **Bob Pullen** – Other than his regular bladder complaints, this Manorfield Close resident is remembered for narrowly escaping death when Eddie hurled an axe in his direction at the 1999 village fête.

Ssshhh!!

✧ **Richard and Sabrina Thwaite** – Part of the fashionable and respectable Grange Spinney set, Sabrina's attractive appearance is often crudely referred to by the laddish Ambridge men. She played the cat in the 2010 production of *Dick Whittington*, in which she was heard mewing with a great deal of emotion – a rare treat for *Archers* listeners. Her husband, Richard, is an accountant.

✦ **Lady Mercedes Goodman** – Wife of the late Sir Sidney Goodman, this Spanish señorita is in mourning for her husband who was knighted for his services to industry – he worked in the food canning business. She enjoys shooting and indulging in some health club pampering.

✦ **Violet Griffiths** – Laurels resident Violet is wife to Peggy Woolley's friend Ted Griffiths, a retired art teacher. She suffers from dementia so isn't fully aware of her husband's devotion to her in her old age.

Ssshhh!!

✦ Other current silent characters include: Lower Loxley's resident falconer, **Jessica**; Ambridge golf club director, **Leigh Barham**; Lily and Freddie's private tutor, **Rosemary Hopwood**; Chris Carter's boss, **Ronnie Grant**; the **Buttons**; Home Farm workers **Andy** and **Jeff**; estate shoot underkeeper, **Pete**; Grey Gables royalist receptionist **Caterina**; Coriander Snell's partner **Jason Bamford**; Lower Loxley bookkeeper **Morag**; wine agent **Nick Parsloe** and Eddie Grundy's old pal **Snatch Foster**.

Ssshhh!!

Gone but not Forgotten:
Betty Tucker

Born: 4 August 1950
Died: 16 December 2005

Farming may have been in her blood, but loyalty and an inherent goodness were in her heart. Betty Tucker arrived in Ambridge in 1974 newly-wed to Mike and stuck with him until her untimely death in 2005, at only fifty-five years old. But Mike didn't make those years easy on her by any means, and often it was Betty's resourcefulness, determination and thick skin that kept her family above water. One of Ambridge's more nomadic families, the Tuckers found themselves transplanted from Rickyard Cottage on Brookfield Farm to Willow Farm where Betty offered bed and breakfast, and then on to the slightly dilapidated Ambridge Farm in 1982. This period saw Betty breeding bees, goats and pedigree sheepdogs before embarking on having babies. After going off the contraceptive pill without Mike's knowledge she fell pregnant with their son Roy, born in 1978, and then gave birth to Brenda in 1981. Two young children, a stressed husband and burgeoning financial difficulties were a lot for Betty to handle, but when Mike was declared bankrupt and their future looked uncertain, she pulled up her bootstraps and accepted a cleaning job for Jennifer Aldridge, cottage thrown in.

Life continued to throw rocks at Betty – she dealt with unwanted advances from employer Brian Aldridge and Mike lost an eye in an accident and sunk into depression. She became the main breadwinner when Jack Woolley offered her a job in the village shop, and worked hard despite her husband's protestations. Eventually she found herself back at Willow Farm after Matthew Thorogood accepted their low offer, funded by the compensation money from Mike's accident. Later life brought some more tragedy – Betty was held hostage in the shop during Clive Horrobin's raid – and thankfully some joy with the marriage of her son Roy to Hayley Jordan and also the birth of his daughter Phoebe (with Kate Madikane), her first grandchild. Betty suffered a heart attack in December 2005. Less than a week later, a second one claimed her life and she was found dead by her life partner, in good times and more importantly in bad times, Mike Tucker.

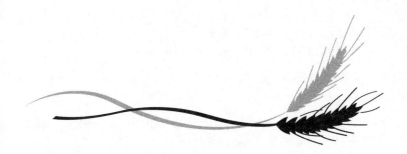

Family Facts: The Grundys

- In 2002 Joe Grundy treated turkey Bathsheba as a pet, and then treated himself to her for Christmas dinner.

- Clarrie paid for her own engagement ring when Eddie proposed.

- When Joe Grundy's wife Susan died he put her personal things in a tin box and stored them in a hayloft on Grange Farm.

- Clarrie gave birth to Ed while visiting her sister Rosie in Great Yarmouth.

- Eddie and Clarrie took part in a 'wife swap' in 2005 to raise money to restore the Cat and Fiddle. They were originally intended to swap with Bert and Freda Fry but ended up switching with Matt and Lilian Bellamy.

- Alf Grundy, Eddie's brother, used to steal chocolate from Woolworths as a boy.

- When forty-something Alf came back to Ambridge briefly in 1986, he stole the contents of nephew Will's money box and his brother's car stereo.

- Ed Grundy went missing in May 2006, and a police investigation followed. He eventually showed up in hospital in July after being beaten up while sleeping rough on the streets of Borchester.

- ✧ Little George Grundy is named after George Barford – Will inherited his gun. His paternity as Will's son, not Ed's, was confirmed by DNA testing.

- ✧ Will Grundy ended his relationship with Nic Hanson after he saw her smack his son George – she reacted when George was squabbling with her daughter Mia. They have since reconciled and now live together at Casa Nueva.

- ✧ Ed and Emma's daughter Keira Susan is the latest edition to the Grundy family, born in April 2011.

Quiz Night at The Bull:

O Come, All Ye Faithful

1   In what year was St Stephen's Church consecrated?
2   Which vicar was instrumental in setting up the football team The Ambridge Wanderers?
3   What was Robin Stokes's other part-time job as well as being a non-stipendiary minister for Ambridge?
4   A vote was held in 1996 to decide the fate of which vicar?
5   Norris Buckland was a controversial vicar who moved to Ambridge for a year in 1955 – where did he come from?
6   Who resigned as church warden over Alan Franks's marriage to Usha Gupta?
7   A memorial window in St Stephens commemorates which Ambridge resident?
8   Name the couple who caused quite a stir in the church when they decided to marry in 1979 because one of them has previously been divorced?
9   In which country did the Reverend Jerry Buckle serve as a lieutenant in the Grenadier Guards?
10 In 1990 what crashed to the floor of the church narrowly missing Will Grundy?

Get to Know the Cast

Bob Arnold was one of two actors who played Doris Archer's brother Tom Forrest, but after his first audition for the programme, Bob was told he would never be on the show due to his recognisable accent, since he had already worked on programmes such as *In the Cotswolds*, *Children's Hour* and other radio plays. Four months later, producers changed their mind and asked him to be part of the programme.

Phillip Molloy (Will Grundy) is the real-life son of Terry Molloy (Mike Tucker) and Heather Barrett, who voiced vicar's wife Dorothy Adamson in the 1970s and 1980s.

Tasmanian-born **Timothy Bentinck** (David Archer) once took some time off working on *The Archers* to help his own father renovate a small farm in Devon – he even helped deliver twin lambs during a snowstorm.

Ballard Berkeley (Colonel Danby) may have played a Colonel on *The Archers* and a Major in *Fawlty Towers* but in reality he spent World War Two working for the Metropolitan Police.

Richard Carrington who played Reverend Richard Adamson, presided over the funeral of Doris Archer for the programme only a week after the death of his own father.

Charles Collingwood and **Judy Bennett** (Brian Aldridge and Shula Hebden Lloyd) married in real life after recording three children's puppet TV shows together. Their off-air relationship has survived Brian's numerous on-air liaisons!

Pamela Craig may have played Mike Tucker's dutiful wife Betty on the programme for many years, but the actress also spent thirteen weeks on Coronation Street as Jackie Marsh, a journalist who had an affair with Ken Barlow.

As Sid Perks, **Alan Devereux** got to keep an eye on his own daughter Tracy-Jane who played Sid's daughter Lucy on the programme.

In the 1980s **Alison Dowling** (Elizabeth Pargetter) was also known for her roles in two other serial dramas – *Crossroads* and *Emmerdale*.

In 2000 **Patricia Gallimore** (Pat Archer) published a book titled *Patricia Gallimore's Organic Year: A Guide to Organic Living*.

When **Patricia Greene** (Jill Archer) joined the programme in 1956 she was so inexperienced in radio acting techniques that when the script called for Jill to pour a cup of coffee over Phil Archer, the actress drenched Norman Painting with a cup of water.

When **Charlotte Martin's** character Susan Carter was put in prison for harbouring her fugitive brother in 1993, the actress was asked to appear on talk show *Kilroy* to discuss women prisoners, but turned down the opportunity because she thought it would blur the line between fact and fiction.

Norman Painting played Phil Archer on the show for nearly sixty years, making him a Guinness World Record holder for the longest continuous performance in the same role. Painting also wrote about 1,200 episodes of the programme under the pseudonym Bruno Milna.

In the 1960s **Angela Piper** (Jennifer Aldridge) used to read the letters for the BBC's *Points of View* programme.

Before **Graham Roberts** stepped into George Barford's boots he played tennis in the qualifying rounds at Wimbledon and rowed in the Henley Royal Regatta.

Teacher **Lesley Saweard** took over the role of Christine Barford after Pamela Mant left the show in the 1950s. She was asked to audition after a chance meeting with Denis Folwell (Jack Archer) when he commented on the similarity of the two actresses' voices.

Colin Skipp was nearly thirty when he auditioned (successfully) for the role of sixteen-year-old Tony Archer.

June Spencer (Peggy Woolley) played both Peggy and Irish lass Rita Flynne in 1951. She took a break from both roles to adopt two children in 1953, and while she returned sporadically a year later to voice the smaller part of Rita, she wouldn't voice Peggy again until 1962.

Haydn Jones, who played Joe Grundy, died on his way to the studio to record an episode of the show in 1984. He was replaced by Edward Kelsey, who for over twenty-five years has made the role indisputably his own and become a firm favourite with listeners.

Welcome to Ambridge: The Vicarage

✧ This four-bedroom bungalow was built in 1974 on the site of the old Georgian Vicarage building.

✧ When Robin Stokes left Ambridge for a new job in Surrey in 1995 he would leave the Vicarage bereft of a vicar until Reverend Alan Franks moved in in 2003. He had lived briefly at the Darrington Vicarage, but it was found to have structural defects.

✧ 1997 saw Dr Richard Locke convert the Vicarage into his surgery practice.

✧ Before it was the village surgery the Church authorities used the Vicarage as a holiday home for underprivileged children.

✧ Now Reverend Alan Franks lives there with his wife Usha; their living room is decorated with a statue of Hindu deity Shiva.

GONE BUT NOT FORGOTTEN:
WALTER GABRIEL

Born: 25 August 1896
Died: 3 November 1988

The large Gabriel family were traditionally the blacksmiths of Ambridge, but Walter went against the grain and was working as a tenant farmer of the Squire in 1951. He bought and sold his farm on, moving to Honeysuckle Cottage. Considered by many to be an inept farmer – neighbour Dan Archer was constantly complaining about his broken fences and dilapidated buildings – Walter was a popular, sociable member of the community whose true vocation was propping up the bar at The Bull. He regularly participated in the Flower and Produce Show and contributed to the village fête.

Having lost his wife Annie at a young age, he invested much of his energy into his son Nelson, who he greatly admired. In Walter's eyes Nelson could do no wrong. Even when Nelson faked his own death to avoid being prosecuted for the Borchester mail van robbery Walter still insisted on his innocence and took his son on a cruise after his acquittal. Nelson's clearly inherited his entrepreneurial spirit from his father, who dabbled in a pet shop, junk shops, a craft studio and a caravan site in his time. Walter provided comic relief for his Ambridge friends and they showed their gratitude when at his ninety-second birthday party he was declared a freeman of The Bull, with Sid Perks announcing all his special ales would be on the house. Despite his determination to go on forever and make the most of Sid's generosity, less than three months later he died of pneumonia.

Making *The Archers*: Sounds like...

Some *Archers* fans are convinced Ambridge is a real place, made up of real houses, a real pub and real barns, stables and vehicles, and it's not hard to hear why. The production of sound effects and sound mixing is a mixture of sophisticated technology and everyday objects to make listeners believe their favourite characters are really rehearsing a pantomime at the village hall, sipping a pint at The Bull or simply relaxing in their kitchen. The show is recorded at the BBC's Birmingham premises at the Mailbox complex in a state-of-the-art studio space. Different areas of the studio produce a variety of acoustics to recreate the aural feel of a small room, a large hall or a pub. There's even a kitchen with all the modern appliances Ambridge families use as well as an AGA cooker. Digital technology means some members of the cast don't need to come to Birmingham to be in the programme. Ten-year-old Ciaran Doyle who plays Ruairi Donovan lives in Dublin and is too young to travel to the studio to record his lines. Instead, a programme assistant travels to Ireland once a month to record his dialogue and it is then seamlessly added to the rest of the cast's conversations.

But the characters in *The Archers* don't spend all their time indoors, so the sound effects artists have a number of clever ways of creating the sounds you'd expect to hear, despite being inside a studio. Actors tread on scrunched up old rolls of tape to record the sound of walking on grass, an old metal ironing board opening and closing stands in for animal pen gates and an Alka-Seltzer dissolving in a glass of water is often used for the sound of champagne bubbles.

Luckily for the *Archers* cast radio means they don't really have to punch each other in the face – they have cabbages for that – and if you get kicked by a cow, as Brian Aldridge once was, you won't have to come face to face with any crazed bovines. Why bother, when a hammer striking a watermelon creates a perfectly suitable sound? Some things in life, however, are far more pleasant. Actors on the show used to kiss their hands when the script called for a smooch between two characters, and it wasn't until 1979, after twenty-eight years of hand-kissing, that Nick Wearing and Shula Archer's actors Gareth Johnson and Judy Bennett shared the first real *Archers* kiss. (It was the introduction of stereo recording made the hand-kissing effects unworkable, as the sound had to come from only one direction, close to the voices!)

Quiz Night at The Bull:

Down on the farm

1 Which farm is responsible for running the Ambridge Organics farm shop?

2 What kind of beef is sold online by David and Ruth Archer?

3 Which farm is home to forty-five Guernsey cows that produce locally sold milk?

4 How many acres was Brookfield Farm when Dan Archer bought it in 1954?

5 Which of Ambridge's farms is the largest with 1,585 arable acres?

6 Which of the following is not a name of one of the fields at Bridge Farm: Queencups, Primrose Bank or Big Leys?

7 What kind of animal is raised organically on Willow Farm?

8 Which family were forced out of Grange Farm due to bankruptcy in 2000?

9 Home farm is home to a maze, but what's it made from?

10 In what year did Dan Archer lose most of his oats when a fire broke out in his Dutch barn?

1 Bridge Farm; 2 Hereford beef; 3 Grange Farm; 4 100 acres; 5 Home Farm; 6 Queencups; 7 Chickens; 8 The Grundys; 9 Maize; 10 1958

124

Ambridge Issues: Racism

It would be wrong to call Ambridge a multi-cultural village, but the introduction of a few out-of-towners of different races and religions have given writers the opportunity to explore issues of racism and prejudice. Usha Gupta (now Franks) – a Ugandan-born Asian solicitor (by way of Coventry) – was the first character to experience the prejudice of some country folk when she was the victim of racist attacks in 1995. She was mugged, had a rock thrown at the window of her cottage and racist slogans and a swastika painted on the walls. Usha almost left Ambridge for good after thugs threw ammonia in her face, leaving her with a corneal abrasion and fear of losing her sight.

Kate Aldridge's father, Brian, revealed more of his own prejudices when his daughter's South African boyfriend Lucas Madikane arrived in Ambridge. Perhaps surprisingly in conservative-minded Ambridge, despite the pair's mixed-race, illegitimate child, the community was very accepting of the polite, educated, charming newcomer and the writers chose not to focus much on Lucas's race, even though he was the first black male character to appear on the programme.

Despite being part of the community since the early 1990s, Hindu Usha faced more problems when she planned to marry the Reverend Alan Franks. The union was a real cause for concern, especially amongst the more stalwart Christians in the village. Shula Hebden Lloyd even went so far as to make disparaging comments in the *Borchester Echo* about the couple's relationship, which led to her resignation as church warden. While church life may not play a huge part in the lives on Ambridge's youth, the parish still fulfils a vital role in the village and for the more religiously fervent members of the community, its presence is paramount.

Welcome to Ambridge: Village Hall

✧ The Village Hall was once the village's own school but has been the home for the playgroup, the WI, the Over Sixties Club, the Flower and Produce Show and many of Lynda Snell's ambitious theatrical productions.

✧ The Hall had a facelift in 1976 after an electrical fire caused damage to the kitchen extension and then a complete refurbishment in 1993 with the help of celebrity project coordinator Anneka Rice.

✧ In 2000 new toilets known as the Jubilee Loos were installed at the Hall after a successful grant application and local fundraising.

✧ Tony Archer and Eddie Grundy held their joint fiftieth birthday celebrations at the Hall in 2009.

✧ Manorfield Close is a cul-de-sac of twelve 'old people's' bungalows opposite the Village Hall. Residents have included Mrs Potter, Mrs Perkins and Colonel Danby.

Not from Round 'Ere

While it's hard to imagine a nicer place to be from than Ambridge, many of the village's residents have been 'incomers', moving to the small Borsetshire haven from all over the globe. Here are just some of the former habitats of Ambridge dwellers.

Majorie Antrobus – Burma; Palestine; Rhodesia; Waterley Cross
Laura Archer – South Otago, New Zealand; Stourhampton
Ruth Archer – Prudhoe, Northumberland
George Barford – Yorkshire
Jeremy Buckle – Nairobi; Derbyshire
Matt Crawford – Peckham
Usha Franks – Kampala, Uganda; Coventry
Cameron Fraser – Scotland
Simon Gerrard – Canada
Siobhan Hathaway – Ireland; London
Martin Lambert – Somerset
Jethro Larkin – Dorset
Richard Locke – Manchester
Lucas Madikane – Langa, Cape Town
Nora McAuley – Ireland
Jolene Perks – Huddersfield
Polly Perks – East End; Penny Hassett
Sid Perks – Birmingham
Paddy Redmond – Northern Ireland
Ellen Rogers – Spain
Lynda Snell –Sunningdale
Oliver Sterling – North Borsetshire
Matthew Thorogood – Papua New Guinea
Martha Woodford – Penny Hassett
Hazel Woolley – Bahamas
Jack Woolley – Stirchley, Birmingham

DANIEL 'DAN' ARCHER

Born: 15 October 1896
Died: 23 April 1986

Considered by many to be the father of *The Archers* as we know it, the legacy of Dan and his wife Doris can be seen in almost all of the programme's current crop of characters. A traditional Borsetshire farmer through and through, Dan came to the profession after a stint in the 16th Battalion of the Borchester Regiment during World War One, after which he returned to his home village of Ambridge and took over the management of Brookfield Farm, previously run by his father, and settled down with Doris. Dan's life would have been considerably different if it weren't for his three children – Jack, Phil and Christine – whose relationships, own families and health problems all added to the drama at Brookfield over the years. With Jack taking up a post as landlord at The Bull, Christine uninterested in running Brookfield and Phil butting heads with his father over modern versus traditional methods, Dan came close to selling up the farm he had worked so hard to buy, believing he would never pass it on to his offspring. Luckily, Phil came around and was able to take over from his father when he retired in 1970.

Through all the ups and downs of life in Ambridge – brother-in-law Tom Forrest's manslaughter trial, the death of son Jack, Christine's unhappy marriage to Paul Johnson and the 1956 foot-and-mouth outbreak that saw all the Brookfield cattle destroyed, one woman was with Dan throughout. His almost-sixty-year marriage to Doris and who knows how many beef and mushroom pies brought Dan true happiness and comfort – something that was hard for him to live without when Doris died in 1980. The loyal family man struggled on for another six years, immersing himself in the lives of his children and grandchildren, but was never quite the same. Dedicated and hard-working to the last, he died of a heart attack while helping a sheep get back on its feet.

Welcome to Ambridge: Village shop

✧ While many villages have seen the disappearance of their local shop or post office in recent years, Ambridge have held on to theirs with a tight fist – the community rallied together in 2010 to save the shop from closure and it is now largely run by volunteers.

✧ Martha Woodford worked as manager and then part-time in the shop spreading gossip for decades. She also introduced an off-licence section and a home-delivery service during her time there.

✧ In 1990 Jack Woolley installed a flashing neon sign, which immediately prompted a village-wide campaign for its removal.

✧ There have been two armed raids on the shop over the years, which must be a higher than average statistic for a peaceful country village.

Village Productions (Act II)

✧ 2004 *A Christmas Carol* – This Lynda Snell production was overshadowed for some Ambridge residents by a dark cloud in the shape of Owen King. When Kathy Perks suggested the seemingly lonely chef take over the role of Mr Fezziwig after Neville Booth dropped out, she couldn't have imagined it would lead to him raping her in the Village Hall. With Kathy traumatised and scared to leave her house, Lynda took over the role, and when Owen King didn't show up for opening night (because Sid had scared him out of Ambridge) Reverend Alan Franks stepped in and gave the part his best shot, much to Lynda's relief.

✧ 2005 *The Spirit of Christmas* – This year's Christmas production was not so much a play, but a festive revue showcasing the best of Ambridge's performing talents. The show was conceived by Julia Pargetter-Carmichael who beat Lynda Snell to booking up the Village Hall at Christmas, much to Lynda's chagrin, and then passed away in November, leaving Lynda to step up and bring the show together. Performances included open-mic comedy from Kenton Archer, a dance performance by Izzy Blake and Pip Archer and 'Frosty the Snowman' sung by the village children.

✧ 2006 *Snow White and the Seven (Slightly Taller Than Average) Dwarves* – This production saw Lynda Snell doing what she does best – bossing people around and chastising them for smoking, missing rehearsals and not taking their roles seriously enough. There was even a revolt of the dwarves at one rehearsal and arguments about who was the tallest dwarf. Opening night saw Chris Carter as 'Teeny' plugging Tom Archer's sausages while the local journalists were witness to some high drama at the press performance when Joe Grundy accidentally set his dwarf beard on fire and had to be extinguished by Brian Aldridge.

✧ 2008 *Jack and the Beanstalk* – Oh, poor Lynda! This year was as difficult as any other with numerous cast members being replaced due to illness and lack of commitment and her frustrations of no one learning their lines on time. Despite all the chopping and changing the opening night was a huge success – even with Mike Tucker's ad-libbing – and in part thanks to Alistair Lloyd's technical effects. Because Eddie Grundy had refused to dance around in the cow costume, Lynda and husband Robert stepped in at the last minute, with Lynda taking the rear end spot. Unfortunately, during the show her hair got caught up in the costume and she had to be cut free from the cow.

✧ 2010 *The Strange Affair at Ambridge Towers* – In addition to the annual Christmas production, 2010 saw more theatrics than usual when the village fête played host to both celebrity guest Colin Dexter and Lynda's complicated murder mystery play. Cast members included Emma Grundy, Jill Archer and a theatrically-challenged David Archer as the policeman. The prize for solving the mystery was two signed Inspector Morse books, which was won by Vicky and Mike Tucker.

✧ 2010 *Dick Whittington* – Rehearsals for this Christmas panto saw Fallon Rogers and milkman Harry Mason making up their own lines and flirting like schoolchildren, much to the annoyance of a jealous Jack 'Jazzer' McCreary. Lynda put on the production especially for her step-grandson Oscar Snell who was happy to meet the cat (played by Sabrina Thwaite) after the show. Felpersham Light Opera Society director Tristram Hawkshaw attended the opening night and wrote a favourable review for the *Echo*.

Quiz Night at The Bull:

Events of the year

1 What colour did Pip Archer dye her hair on April Fool's Day to wind up her parents?
2 Whose jawbone was found in the village pond in 1990?
3 In what year did The Bull open a Civil War-themed restaurant?
4 Who led the Ambridge Scout Troop in the 1970s?
5 Which Archer dressed as Superman for the County Hotel's fancy dress ball in 1983?
6 Who scooped a record fifteen first prizes at the 1985 Flower and Produce Show?
7 What was Elizabeth wearing when she came third in the 1986 Penny Hassett pancake race?
8 What did Shula Hebden Lloyd bet Alistair he wouldn't be able to give up for Lent in 2000?
9 Who represented Ambridge's WI at a Buckingham Palace garden party in 1965?
10 Who played Scrooge in Lynda Snell's production of *A Christmas Carol*?

1 Blue; 2 Florrie Hoskins's; 3 1995; 4 Phil Archer; 5 Tony; 6 Pru Forrest; 7 A French maid's outfit; 8 Alcohol; 9 Doris Archer; 10 Joe Grundy

134

Welcome to Ambridge: Willow Farm

✧ In 1972 Haydn Evans bought this full working farm for his son Gwyn. The land has since been divided and sold off over time to Phil Archer, Brian Aldridge and Bill Insley.

✧ The farm house is now divided into two properties: Willow Farm where Roy and Hayley Tucker live with their two daughters, and adjoining Willow Cottage where Roy's father, Mike, lives with his second wife Vicky.

✧ There is a memorial apple tree for Mike's late first wife, Betty, in the garden.

✧ Eight acres of Willow Farm land are now owned by Neil Carter who has an outdoor herd of breeding sows and an organic free-range egg business.

✧ Neil Carter, with Mike's help, built wife Susan her dream house – Ambridge View – on his plot of Willow Farm land.

Gone but not Forgotten:
Siobhan Hathaway
(née Donovan)

Born: 13 June 1965
Died: 31 May 2007

When Siobhan arrived in Ambridge from London in 1999 – the wife of the new village doctor, Tim Hathaway – and fell in love with the quaint countryside village and adorable Honeysuckle Cottage, it's unlikely anyone pigeonholed her as a husband-snatching adulteress. As it turned out, Siobhan ended up being at the centre of one of *The Archers'* most controversial and long-running storylines. A translator by trade, Siobhan struggled to adjust to the gossipy nature of communication adopted by the village, especially when her miscarriage became common knowledge. She soon adjusted to village life, however, and became good friends with Elizabeth Archer. A new job working for a publisher saw her travelling more and more and indirectly encouraged her husband to pursue his feelings for the vicar, Janet Fisher.

The couple's stressful Christmas in 2000 was the setting for Tim's kiss with Janet; he also gave her a scarf he'd previously given to an ungrateful Siobhan who said it wasn't her colour. The dalliance didn't progress after Siobhan confronted him, but it was enough to push her into the arms of Brian Aldridge. After an affair that resulted in Siobhan becoming pregnant, and despite Brian's love for Siobhan, he chose to stay with wife Jennifer, and with her own marriage in tatters Siobhan fled to Germany. She reverted to her maiden name, Donovan, and began a relationship with Dieter. Her son Ruairi was born in 2002 and although Brian kept in regular contact, visiting his son secretly on supposed business trips to Hungary, the couple did not reunite. In April 2007, Siobhan revealed to Brian that she was suffering from advanced malignant melanoma and asked him to raise Ruairi if she died. She succumbed to the disease weeks later knowing Ambridge's most controversial baby would return to the village to be with his father.

Family Facts: The Horrobins

✧ Three of Bert and Ivy Horrobin's six children have spent time at Her Majesty's pleasure: Clive, Keith and Susan.

✧ Clive Horrobin was caught trespassing in the Country Park when he was eleven.

✧ Pinky, the pig Susan Horrobin won at the village fête in 1983, brought Neil Carter close to Susan – he helped her care for the pig.

✧ Tracy Horrobin was the bridesmaid at sister Susan's wedding to Neil.

✧ Clive Horrobin abandoned girlfriend Sharon Richards and his new baby Kylie six weeks after she was born.

✧ Despite convictions for armed robbery and grievous bodily harm, Clive's mother Ivy continued to support him and visit him in prison.

✧ Bert Horrobin works in road maintenance and enjoys drinking, smoking and playing cards.

Making *The Archers*: Front page news

Whether it's celebrity appearances – such as Camilla, Duchess of Cornwall's recent cameo on the show – or anniversary episodes, *The Archers* storylines have been finding their way into the British papers for over sixty years. Dedicated *Archers* fans have become rather attached to the characters in Ambridge and that attachment is never more obvious than when something truly tragic and terrible happens to the Borsetshire bunch they've come to know and love. The earliest high-profile example of the programme making the news was Grace Archer's death in 1955. The headline-grabbing story, which saw Phil's new wife trapped in a burning barn, aired on the night commercial broadcaster ITV first went on air, and afterwards letters of mourning flooded into the BBC. The story made the front page of some papers and the *Daily Express* demanded 'Why do this to Grace Archer?' The production team decided not to broadcast the funeral as they were concerned too many wreaths would be delivered to the studio. A similar outpouring of grief and shock occurred when Shula's husband Mark Hebden died in a car accident, made even more shocking by *Archers* editor Vanessa Whitburn's own near-fatal car crash a week before Mark's.

Death alone is not the only thing to get listeners and journalists all fired up. One of the programme's most publicised stories was the imprisonment of Susan Carter after she harboured her bad-boy brother Clive Horrobin, on the run for committing a mail van robbery in 1993. Hailed as the Ambridge One by fans (in reference to the miscarriages of justice over the Guildford Four and the Birmingham Six), a fan-led campaign to see her released was soon underway, with Home Secretary Michael Howard joining in the debate. The newspapers lapped up the story with petitions and sensational headlines. Despite public pressure, Susan remained in prison from 23 December 1993 until 31 March. Jenny Webb, the fan who kicked off the campaign by producing posters exclaiming 'Free the Ambridge One!', wanted to draw attention to the fact many women are imprisoned unfairly or too severely for their crimes, leaving families in tatters and children motherless.

Welcome to Ambridge: Woodbine Cottage

✧ Situated next door to The Bull and opposite the village green, Woodbine was once a tied property owned by Brookfield Farm.

✧ Mabel and Ned Larkin were the Archers' first tenants at Woodbine Cottage, although Ned died shortly after moving in in 1967.

✧ The cottage was bought by Christine Barford and her husband George after their previous home was petrol-bombed by arsonist Clive Horrobin.

✧ Bert and Freda Fry used to live here, but relocated to Brookfield Bungalow when a lorry skidded off the road destroying part of the cottage.

✧ Next door to Woodbine is Jim Lloyd's home Greenacres. It was built on the site of the Old Police House, which was destroyed in an arson attack.

Quiz Night at The Bull:

Departures and departed

1. What object was Arthur Tovey holding that touched a power cable causing his death in 1976?
2. Whose car was Janet Tregorran in when she died?
3. Christine's first husband, Paul Johnson, died in a car crash in which country?
4. Polly Perks was killed when a tanker skidded into her car – what was in the tanker?
5. Which gamekeeper shot himself in the shepherd's hut in the woods in 2004?
6. How many weeks were there between the deaths of Julia Pargetter and Betty Tucker?
7. Who spent their last days at a clinic in Scotland due to liver failure and passed away in 1972?
8. Who were the two people to find George Barford just in time when he had taken an overdose in 1974?
9. Who died after a family tea party at Glebe Cottage asleep in her chair in 1980?
10. Ralph Bellamy died after suffering a second heart attack in 1980 and had a memorial service in Ambridge, but where was his funeral held?

1 Aluminium ladder; 2 Charles Grenville's; 3 Germany; 4 Milk; 5 Greg Turner; 6 Six; 7 Jack Archer; 8 Tom and Pru Forrest; 9 Doris Archer; 10 Guernsey

Archers Extra

Not getting enough from your weekly *Archers* doses? Take a look at some of these websites, books and audio filled with even more wonderful *Archers* information.

Websites

The BBC Archers home page
http://www.bbc.co.uk/radio4/features/the-archers/
The official site for the programme, affectionately known as 'Mustardland' due to its slightly garish colour scheme, with family trees, character profiles, message boards and a timeline of key events in the series.

Ambridge Village
http://www.ambridgevillage.co.uk/
This official BBC blog is written from the perspectives of the residents of Ambridge. It'll keep you informed of upcoming events and activities in the village and help you get to know your favourite characters a little better.

The Archers Addicts
http://www.thearchers.co.uk/
The official fan club with a shop, news features, a blog and a discussion forum.

Saddicts
http://www.saddicts.com/
Comprehensive tongue-in-cheek information on the history and geography of Ambridge, with a particularly thorough listing of the history of each of the most significant buildings in the village.

The Archers Anarchists
http://www.archersanarchists.com/
The @rchers @narchists know the real truth behind *The Archers*:
it's not a serial drama, as so many of us believe, but a fly-on-
the-wall documentary about 'a village inhabited by social misfits,
murderers and nauseatingly cosy people'. This site is cynical,
twisted and very, very funny.

Borsetshire Families
http://www.squiresfamily.me.uk/archers/borsetshire/
A useful clickable database showing relationships between
Ambridge residents past and present.

The Archers Plot Summaries
http://www.lowfield.co.uk/archers/
Short summaries of life in Ambridge in a particular year, month
or episode.

Pondering The Archers
http://ponderingthearchers.blogspot.com/
In its author's words, this blog is an 'unofficial meander through
every episode of *The Archers*' going back to January 2010, with
key quotes and commentary.

Books

The Archers Archives
Simon Frith and Chris Arnot
Looking back over sixty years of the programme, scriptwriter Frith
and journalist Arnot relive some of the programme's defining
moments, with behind-the-scenes exclusives and cast interviews.

Who's Who in the Archers 2011
Graham Harvey
The BBC's annual A–Z round-up of all Ambridge's current residents is a wonderful refresher for an *Archers* fan and a great character introduction for any new listener.

Jennifer Aldridge's Archers' Cookbook
Angela Piper
With over 150 recipes this season-by-season tour of all of Ambridge's kitchens – from Jennifer's perspective – means you can make Lilian's rich tiramisu without having to pop round for tips.

The Archers Miscellany
Joanna Toye
Full of delightful titbits from the lives of Ambridge's finest, this little compendium will have you reminiscing about episodes gone by and learning some things you probably never knew about those country folk.

Audio

The Best of Vintage Archers
Relive some of the programme's classic moments with this collection of clips from vintage *Archers* storylines.

Ambridge Affairs: Love Triangles
Experience the drama all over again with these collections of episodes featuring Sid Perks's steamy affair and subsequent marriage to Jolene and Emma Carter's turmoil over the two Grundy brothers.

Ambridge Affairs: Heartache at Home Farm
The defining moment of the Aldridges' marriage – Brian's relationship with Siobhan Hathaway – can be unravelled in its entirety with this collection of adulterous episodes.